THE ENGLISH LANGUAGE TEACHER'S HANDBOOK

The
English Language Teacher's Handbook

How to teach large classes with few resources

Joanna Baker and
Heather Westrup

Sharing skills. Changing lives

continuum
LONDON • NEW YORK

Continuum   **VSO**
The Tower Building   370 Lexington Avenue   317 Putney Bridge Road
11 York Road   New York   London
London SE1 7NX   NY 10017–6503   SW15 2PN
www.continuumbooks.com

First published by Continuum in 2000
Reprinted 2002, 2003

British Library Cataloguing-in-Publication Data
A catalogue record for this book is available from the British Library.

ISBN 0–8264-4787-2 (paperback)

Illustrations:
2.1, 8.1, 8.3, 12.5, 15.3, 17.1, 19.9 by Dandi Palmer © VSO/Dandi Palmer
6.1, 12.4, 17.2, 19.1, 19.2, 19.10, 20.2 © Caroline Burnley

Typeset by Kenneth Burnley, Wirral, Cheshire
Printed and bound in Great Britain by Creative Print and Design, Ebbw Vale, Wales

Contents

Acknowledgements

The authors would like to thank their overseas colleagues in Europe, Africa and Asia, VSO teachers overseas and their national colleagues, and VSO trainers in the UK. All of them have contributed ideas over the years on which much of this book is based. Without their creativity and ability to face the challenge of teaching large classes with few resources, and their willingness to share their ideas, this book could not have been written. We would also like to thank the staff of VSO Books for their hard work, enthusiasm and encouragement.

The authors are grateful to Simon Haines and to Thomas Nelson & Sons Ltd for permission to reproduce part of their book *Projects for the EFL Classroom*.

This book reflects 40 years of VSO experience of teaching English in developing countries and Eastern Europe, including Bangladesh, Cambodia, China, Egypt, Eritrea, Ethiopia, Gambia, Ghana, Guinea Bissau, Guyana, Indonesia, Kenya, Lao PDR, Malawi, Maldives, Mongolia, Mozambique, Namibia, Nepal, Nigeria, Pakistan, Poland, Russia, Solomon Islands, Sri Lanka, Tanzania, Uganda, Vietnam, Zambia and Zimbabwe.

1 / Introduction

This book is for teachers of English who teach large classes with few resources. It contains many ideas to help you in your teaching. It will show you how to make teaching and learning English easier and more interesting for yourself and your students. It will help you to think about how you teach now and how to extend and improve your teaching methods.

Some ministries of education, and teachers too, want to introduce changes in the way English is taught. They would like students to be more motivated and successful. One way of doing this is to encourage students to participate more in the learning process. This book gives plenty of examples of what you can do and how you can incorporate these ideas into your classroom.

This book does not suggest that you change your teaching method completely. We suggest that you start by trying one or two of the activities in the book. If they work in your classroom, try other activities. As you extend your teaching method, you and your students will become used to the new ideas and changes. You may be able to see that they are having a positive effect on your students' language ability and motivation to learn English. Then you can continue to add more ideas from this book throughout the year to teach your course or syllabus.

This book reflects the learning and experience of VSO teachers and their national colleagues, teaching English in a wide range of developing countries and in Eastern Europe. The practical teaching approaches, ideas and activities in this book were contributed by VSO teachers and national English teachers working in countries throughout the developing world, including Bangladesh, People's Republic of Congo, China, Cameroon, Eritrea, Ghana, Nepal, Nigeria, Pakistan and St Vincent. Many of these teachers work in schools with few resources, and many of them teach very large classes. Whether you are a new or experienced teacher, you can use the activities and ideas in this book to help you strengthen your teaching and help your students to learn better.

WHY IS ENGLISH TEACHING IMPORTANT?

Teaching English is an important job. Many governments and ministries of education believe that it is important for students to learn English. In many countries, secondary school and university courses are taught in English, and English is one of the main languages of national communication and business. English is also one of the most important international languages. It gives access to information, for example, in the areas of business, finance, science, medicine and technology. Students who become fluent in English can have the opportunity to contribute to the development of their country.

So, as an English teacher, you have a valuable and worthwhile job. This book will support you in the challenges you face; but first, let's look at some of the challenges.

THE CHALLENGES OF A LARGE CLASS

A class is large if the teacher feels that there are too many students for them all to make progress in English. So a large class can mean any number! However, it is not just the number of students which makes teaching difficult. In large classes, there may be big differences in the students' ability. Many large classes also have the following characteristics:

► desks and chairs are fixed or difficult to move;
► students sit close together in rows;
► there is little space for the teacher to move around the classroom;
► there is not enough space for students to move during the lesson;
► the walls between classrooms are thin, and any noise will disturb other classes;
► there are not enough textbooks for all students;
► not every student has paper and pencil;
► the school has no copying facilities;
► other teaching resources are limited.

This means that teachers and students can face the following challenges:

► teachers can have difficulty keeping everyone's attention;
► students' motivation to learn English can be poor;
► students have difficulty hearing the teacher;
► teachers do not have enough opportunity to help weaker students;

▶ attendance can be poor and irregular, leading to lack of continuity;
▶ this lack of continuity can cause extra work for teachers and confusion for students;
▶ taking the register can be time-consuming;
▶ teachers can have too much marking to do;
▶ there are few resources to make learning interesting.

WHAT ARE RESOURCES?

Resources are anything which the teacher uses to help students learn. Many teachers have few resources, perhaps only a blackboard and a few books. The school may not have technical resources such as tape recorders, radios, television sets, video players or computers.

In this book, you will see how teachers of large classes all over the world have developed creative ideas for using the blackboard. They have found ways to use anything, inside or outside the classroom, as a resource for teaching and learning. They have developed ways to teach English in an interesting and motivating way with these resources.

This book gives many ideas for overcoming the challenges of a large class with few resources. It suggests different ways of teaching English which make learning more effective.

Let's look at some of the different ways of teaching English.

A BRIEF OVERVIEW OF WAYS TO TEACH ENGLISH

There is no single way to learn English. Throughout the world, millions of students are learning English in many ways and in many different language contexts. Some students see and hear English every day outside school, so they begin to understand and use English almost effortlessly. Other students only see English in books at school, and their teacher may not speak much English, so it is more difficult for them to learn to use English.

Students also have different reasons for learning English. They may learn English

▶ because all other subjects in school are taught in English;
▶ because English is a compulsory subject;
▶ in order to pass national or university exams;
▶ because they know that being able to use English can lead to a better job;
▶ for pleasure and personal interest.

These reasons affect the students' motivation to learn English.

Students also have different ways of learning. Some students

- ▶ like to write everything down and study it carefully;
- ▶ are worried when they make a mistake;
- ▶ do not worry about grammar and use English at every opportunity, both in and out of the classroom;
- ▶ do not like to speak in class;
- ▶ like to study grammar;
- ▶ are good at imitating sounds and words;
- ▶ are good at remembering lists of words.

All these differences mean that many different learning and teaching methods can be effective. Three of the main teaching methods are:

1. Grammar Translation;
2. Direct Methods;
3. Communicative Language Teaching.

How do these methods differ?

Grammar Translation

In the Grammar Translation method, students study grammar and learn lists of vocabulary in order to translate texts. In the classroom, the teacher uses the students' first or main language to explain the grammar and vocabulary in the text and then helps the students to translate it. This method is based on the idea that language is made up of words (vocabulary) and that language changes according to rules (grammar). When students know the rules of grammar and enough words, they can then read and write well in English. This method is very useful for academic work and for passing written exams, but it is less useful if students need to use English in everyday life.

Direct Methods

The two main ways of teaching which make up the Direct Methods are the Audio-lingual Method, which emphasises repetition, and the Audio-visual Method, in which repetition is based on a visual stimulus (like an object or a drawing). Both methods are based on the idea that all skills improve with practice. Language is made up of the skills of reading, listening, writing and speaking, and students learn English by practising these skills. Direct Methods aim to help students use

English in everyday situations rather than learning about grammar and vocabulary to translate texts.

Both Direct methods strongly emphasise the skills of speaking and listening. Writing and reading are considered less important. In the classroom, teachers and learners try to speak English all the time. Translation is discouraged. Students improve their language skills by practising responses to the teacher's prompts or cues. In this way, students can memorise phrases and dialogues. Language laboratories are an effective teaching aid for students learning to listen and repeat in this way.

The Direct Methods are excellent for helping students say sentences correctly and pronounce English well.

Some of the limitations of these methods are:

▶ students may not always understand what they are repeating;
▶ students cannot make their own responses in new and different situations;
▶ teachers may not be confident enough to use English throughout the lesson;
▶ they are not so useful for advanced learners.

Communicative Language Teaching

Communicative Language Teaching is based on the way children learn their first language. Small children slowly learn to use language correctly as they get older. They use the words and language they have already learned and gradually improve the way they communicate in their everyday life. Children make mistakes as they learn to use language.

In the classroom, the teacher sets different tasks and activities to encourage the students to communicate in English, using the language they have already learnt (inside or outside the classroom). For example, they exchange information, discuss and solve problems in pairs or groups. Sometimes students struggle to understand and be understood, but this is part of the learning process. The teacher does not always correct mistakes. The students' English improves the more they use it, in the same way as children learn language.

Communicative methods work best if

▶ the teacher uses realistic activities based on situations which students experience in their lives;

► the teacher sets tasks and problems which interest and motivate the students;

► the teacher includes everyday materials, such as newspapers, timetables, etc., in the tasks.

This method works well if students bring a lot of English to the classroom from the outside world. In places where the teacher is the only source of English, the students may not have enough English to perform these communication tasks and activities. They may need a lot of help and can become demotivated. The teacher may need to give more guided practice and teach grammar and vocabulary first, to enable students to do these communication activities.

HOW THIS BOOK CAN HELP YOU

As we have seen, there are many ways of teaching and learning English. The effectiveness of each teaching method depends on your situation and on the needs of your students: do they need to write essays, pass grammatical tests, or listen to and speak English in their everyday lives?

We believe that using activities from a variety of teaching methods helps students to learn better. This is because using different approaches, activities and materials makes learning more interesting and gives all students an opportunity to make progress. It also means that you can incorporate new ideas gradually, starting with what is familiar and slowly introducing new methods. For example, you can introduce a new way of presenting new vocabulary (see Chapter 6). You can make text into dialogues which students can memorise (Direct Method) or students could act out some of the situations in the book or debate some of the issues in the text (Communicative Language Teaching). You will find plenty of ideas and activities in this book which will help you introduce these kind of changes.

Teaching English to a large class with few resources can be a difficult job. You may feel that it is difficult to try out new teaching methods and ideas, like encouraging students to use the language they learn and to participate in the lesson. This is where this book will help you.

We have written this book to help you to choose teaching approaches and activities which you can use in your classroom to make your teaching more effective and to help your students learn better. We believe that if a teacher uses a variety of teaching approaches and activities, all students have a chance to learn English better.

We do not suggest radical changes. This is because the teaching method you use now probably reflects your students' needs and the accepted ways of teaching in your school. For example, you understand what students expect from you as their teacher and what you expect of your students. You know the normal teaching methods and procedures in a classroom in your country. You know about these conditions, and only you can decide which new ideas would be acceptable. So we suggest that you start by trying out one or two new ideas. If they are successful, you can build on this and gradually introduce more.

Many of the ideas in this book will help students to use English and to take a more active part in the lessons. Once students get used to being more involved during lessons, they become more motivated to learn. When they are motivated to learn, they usually become more successful at English.

This book is divided into chapters:

In Chapter 2 we suggest ways of introducing new ideas and methods to your students, to other members of staff and to other people involved in the way your students learn.

In Chapter 3 we look at some different views of language. We will see how these influence the methods and teaching materials used in the classroom.

In Chapters 4 and 5 we look at how to organise a basic English lesson to teach new language and to practise reading, listening, writing and speaking.

Chapter 6 to 15 contain many practical ideas and activities for teaching English. You can also read about how to do a role play and project work, how to help your students give presentations and how you can write and organise tests. These chapters will be particularly interesting to you if you are looking for ways of adding variety and interest to your existing teaching method.

Chapters 16 to 18 give detailed practical advice on techniques for planning and classroom management. They give lots of examples of how to organise and manage a large class to help you put these techniques into practice. The techniques will encourage students to participate, even when there are few resources.

Chapters 19 and 20 are full of ideas on how to manage what resources you have in a large class and how to add to your resources.

Some chapters have a Classroom Action Task for you to do. These help you to think about how you can use the new teaching ideas and put them into practice with your classes in school. Try out the tasks in your classroom. Use a notebook to record your answers and comments. Remember to make a note of how the new idea or activity worked, and what you could change to make it more suitable for your own teaching context. This notebook will be your Teacher's Action Diary. If you are studying with other teachers, you can discuss the Action Tasks in pairs or groups.

Classroom Action Task

Which of the three methods is used in the English classes you teach? Why do you think this method is used?

Think about three students in your class who are good at learning English. Write down why you think they learn so well (see the list on page 4).

Now think about three students who have problems learning English. Why do you think they are not so successful?

Make a list of four things you would like to change about the way you teach English. Write down some ideas about what you hope to do to make these changes happen.

2/ Introducing Change

In this chapter we suggest ways to help you introduce new ideas and methods to your students, to other members of staff and to other people who are involved in the way your students learn.

WHY CHANGE THE WAY YOU TEACH?

First of all, let's think about the reasons why teachers may want to change the way they teach.

Some teachers *have to* introduce changes in the way they teach because

► the ministry of education wants to introduce Communicative Language Teaching or other new methods in English language learning;
► a new course book has been introduced;
► a different kind of syllabus has been introduced;
► exams have changed;
► economic or political changes in your country mean that students need to communicate in English as well as being able to translate texts.

Other teachers *want to* make changes in the way they teach because

► they want to improve the motivation and achievement of their students;
► they believe that students learn better when they participate actively in the lesson;
► they like to keep up to date and try out new ideas and methods.

You will need to think about what these changes will mean for you and your classroom teaching. Look at these three pictures (Figure 2.1).

Figure 2.1

You can see that there is a very big difference between what teachers do in the classroom when they use different teaching methods such as Grammar Translation method, Direct Methods or Communicative Language Teaching. In Figure 2.1A, the teacher is explaining grammar to the whole class. In Figure 2.1B, the teacher is conducting a drill with the class divided in two. In Figure 2.1C, the teacher is monitoring while the students communicate with each other in groups. In A, the students are sitting and listening to the teacher. In B and C, the students are participating in the lesson and using different kinds of materials to help them learn to use the language. They are more active than in A: the classroom is a busier and probably a noisier place. As we shall see later, this can be a positive learning situation.

Table 2.1 summarises some useful information about the role of the teacher and the students in the three teaching methods we examined in Chapter 1.

Table 2.1

	Role of the teacher	Task of the student
Grammar Translation	Supplier of knowledge	To listen To take notes To translate texts
Direct Methods	Conductor Organiser Model of language	To repeat and practise To memorise language To practise changes
Communicative Language Teaching	Organiser of learning Facilitator	To experiment with the language To take part in activities using English

ADAPTING CHANGES TO YOUR OWN ENVIRONMENT

When you plan to introduce changes in the classroom, you should first think carefully about the context in which you teach. Think about your school, the people involved inside and outside the classroom (such as other teachers and parents) and the resources that you have. Also think about the course that you teach. What do your students need to achieve? Are there exams? If so, what kind?

This book has many suggestions and ideas which have been introduced successfully by teachers who have worked in classrooms like yours. If you want try out new ideas, you should select those ideas which are most appropriate for your own teaching environment. Sometimes, the success of a new idea depends on how confident you are that it will work, so begin with an idea you can do with confidence.

When introducing new ideas:

▶ introduce changes gradually over several months;
▶ find ways of explaining to everyone, both in and out of the classroom, why you are changing the way you teach;
▶ select activities which meet your students' needs (for example, if your students have to pass exams);
▶ start with an activity which is short, motivating and easy for you to manage;
▶ prepare the activity and the resources you need very carefully;
▶ give very clear, step-by-step instructions, and write these on the blackboard;
▶ and most important – if an activity in this book is not successful the first time for you and your class, do not give up – try another one.

Let's look at some ways in which you can help other people understand why you are teaching in a different way.

INTRODUCING CHANGES TO STUDENTS

► Introduce your students to the idea of English for communication (there are some suggestions on how to do this below).

► Tell your students (in their first language if possible) that you are going to try some different activities in class, and explain why.

► Agree a written contract with your students about participation and using English in the classroom. Write this on a poster and keep it at the front of the room.

► Tell your students very clearly what you expect of them the first time you do an activity, and give them clear instructions.

► Spend most of the lesson doing what you normally do and introduce very small changes. Start with a short and simple activity.

► Make very small demands on your students.

► Make sure the new activity is successful and interesting so that students are motivated to want more.

► Introduce the changes over several months.

INTRODUCING CHANGES TO TEACHERS AND OTHERS

When you introduce a different way of teaching, there may be doubts from parents, head teachers, other teachers and even inspectors. Many people are used to students who sit quietly, listen to the teacher and either take notes or copy from the blackboard. They may not be used to students participating in class by doing activities. This is why you must inform these people about the changes you are going to make in your teaching and explain why you think the changes will help students learn better.

Here are some ways you and your students can help other people understand the changes you intend to introduce.

► Write a letter with your students, in your own language, to other teachers explaining your new methods. Tell other teachers what you are trying to do, and why.

► Students can make a poster which explains what is happening in their English class, and display this in the school.

► Share your new ideas and materials with other teachers.

► If your students are advanced enough to do presentations or debates, invite other staff to come along and watch. Send invitations and put posters up to advertise this event.

Classroom Action Task

Prepare one of the following activities and try it out with your students, using your first language. Discuss it with your students. Afterwards, make notes in your Teacher's Action Diary on how your students reacted to the activity. Discuss this with your colleagues.

These activities will show students the idea of learning English for communication.

1. Write a letter from someone who is studying in an English-speaking country, for example, a university student. Read it to your students. Then ask them to discuss how the writer's knowledge of English has helped him or her. They can discuss what the writer needed to be able to do in English in order to study (for example, fill in an application form, understand what the university teachers are saying in English, write well in English, speak English to make friends, and so on). *Or:* Pretend that you are someone in your town who has a job in which you need to speak and use good English. Ask students to interview you about how much English you need to do this job and how you learned it. You can say that you wish you had studied harder at school and that you wish you had had a chance to speak in class.

2. Translate a short text with your students. Then read out a few sentences or a short dialogue, either in English or in your first language. Ask students to listen to the dialogue and discuss where the conversation is taking place and who is speaking.

For example, 'Excuse me, can you tell me where the bookshop is?'

'This is Peter. He will be working with us for six months'.

Compare the two activities with your students. Discuss why it is useful to know and understand real-life language in conversations, and to be able to communicate in English, rather than just translate text.

3 / Background to Teaching English

In this chapter we look at different views about language and how people learn, and how these influence the teaching methods and the teaching materials that we use in the classroom. At the end of the chapter, we will show you how to analyse your course so you can plan to use a variety of teaching methods and activities.

VIEWS OF LANGUAGE

For a long time, there has been a lot of discussion about how languages are used and learnt. Until the middle of the twentieth century, many people believed that, in order to speak or write the best kind of English, you had to use complete sentences which were grammatically correct. People learning English wanted to learn to write and speak this 'Standard English'. They also wanted to sound like native speakers of English from the Home counties. Two things have happened to change these ideas.

First, English has become an international language and it is used as the main language or one of the main languages in countries like America, Australia, India, Malaysia, Nigeria, Pakistan, Philippines, Singapore, South Africa, Zambia and Zimbabwe.

In these countries, different varieties of English have developed. People may pronounce English differently and they may use a different sentence structure from Standard English. Similar words may have completely different meanings or they may not exist in Standard English. For example, in Ghana, people use the word 'trek' to mean 'walk': 'I trekked to the shop on the corner.' 'Trek' also exists in Standard English, but it has a much more specific meaning than 'walk' (it means to migrate or to make a long and difficult journey on foot, carrying equipment and camping at night). But people speaking local varieties of English have no problems communicating with other people who speak the same variety. However, these different or local varieties of English can sometimes be a problem for teachers. Your students may be fluent in the local variety of English, but in order to understand their textbooks or pass their exams they may have to learn British English or American English. (This book is written in British English.)

Second, people need a common language in order to communicate with each other – for business, travel and social reasons. So, some linguists began to think more about how people actually use and learn to use language for communication in real everyday life.

These changes mean that we now analyse language in several different ways. Let's look at the most notable of these views of language: the Grammatical View (sometimes called the Structural View) and the Functional View. Figure 3.1 gives you more information about some of the different areas of these two views.

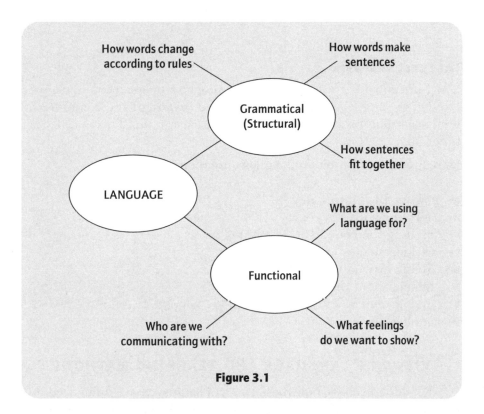

Figure 3.1

The Grammatical View

The Grammatical View is based on the idea that language consists of words (vocabulary) and grammar. Words change according to certain rules, and grammar puts the words into the correct order by following certain rules. When students know the words and understand the rules of grammar, then the meaning of the language becomes clear. Then, students can create an endless variety of sentences and it is possible to translate from one language to another easily. In order to study grammar, students need to know the labels which describe different kinds of words (parts of speech) and their place in a sentence (grammatical function). Have a look at the sentence following:

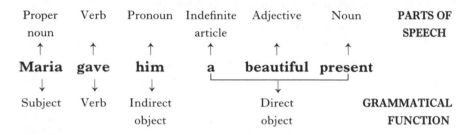

The Functional View

The Functional View is based on analysing how people use language. It categorises language depending upon the *context* of the communication, according to what we are using language to do. This is called its function.

Here are some examples of language functions:

► asking for information;
► agreeing with someone;
► inviting someone to do something;
► making suggestions;
► giving instructions;
► talking about the future;
► giving advice;
► apologising.

VIEWS OF LANGUAGE AND TEACHING METHODS

It is not difficult to see how these views of language have influenced our teaching methods. There is a very close link between the Grammatical View of describing language and the Grammar Translation method of teaching it. Teachers who teach using this method need to have a wide knowledge of vocabulary, a good knowledge of sentence structure and of how texts are formed. Teachers need to know how to describe all this to students in their first or main language. Teachers and students use translation to understand the meaning of a text, so lessons focus mainly upon reading texts and writing down the translation.

The Functional View of language looks at *how* people use language to communicate. The meaning of the language is usually clear because of the context in which the language is used. You can see how the Direct Methods, with the emphasis on memorising phrases and dialogues, and Communicative Language Teaching, with the emphasis on communication, are related to this view of language.

Many teachers use a combination of all three methods (as we shall see in Chapters 4 and 5). We have written this book to support you in using a variety of these methods and activities in your classroom.

WHY WE LABEL LANGUAGE

Why is it useful for teachers to know about these different ways of analysing and labelling language? We have seen how the different views of language affect the teaching methods which teachers use in the classroom.

Most courses are constructed with a particular view of language in mind. For example, we might have a grammatical syllabus, where language is taught through a series of grammar learning points, or a course book in which the activities are strongly functional. Exams, too, are sometimes written with a particular view in mind.

It is not easy for teachers who have a functional course book to help students who need to pass an exam which tests their knowledge of grammar or ability to translate. Students can have a conversation in English, but they cannot identify and label parts of speech or grammatical functions.

In the same way, students may need to learn English so they can communicate in their everyday life, but their textbooks only teach about English grammar. So they can translate literature but they cannot ask the way to a bus stop. Teachers who know about these ways of analysing language can make sure that they use a variety of teaching methods to meet their students' needs.

So now let's look at how we can analyse our syllabus or course books and how to deal with this kind of mismatch between needs and methods.

LOOKING AT COURSE BOOKS

First, you need to look at your course book to identify which view of language it reflects. Here are some examples of exercises and classroom activities from different course books. They show you how a view of language is reflected in a classroom activity. Try to identify the language views and teaching method for each (the answers follow).

Example 1

Write the comparative of these adverbs in each blank.

1. hard   If she doesn't study _____, she'll never pass the exam.

2. well   He plays football _____ than his brother.

3. fast   Amina runs _____ than Abbas.

4. quiet   Kai Lian spoke _____ than Hai Bee.

(*Answer*: Structural View and Grammar Translation teaching method. You can see that students need to know the labels for grammar and parts of speech ('comparative', 'adverbs') and that there is no wider context to the language.)

Example 2

Students in Group A: You are customers at the market. Go from stall to stall and complain politely about the following goods that you bought:

1. A bag. The handle is loose.
2. A bicycle pump. The part which attaches it to the bike is missing.
3. A clock. It loses ten minutes a day.

Students in Group B: You sold these goods in the market. Be polite to each customer and try to be as helpful as possible.

(*Answer*: Functional View. You can see that students are given a real-life situation as the context for the language. The function of the language in this activity is to communicate a complaint.)

DIFFERENT VIEWS IN A SINGLE COURSE BOOK

You may find that your course book contains exercises and activities which reflect different views of language and teaching methods. Look at this typical part of the contents page (or 'menu') from a recent course book (Figure 3.2). We have labelled the activities and language areas with the different views of language.

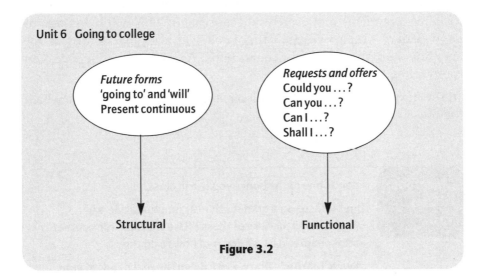

Figure 3.2

By including a variety of activities, the courses expose the students to a range of methods of learning and views about language. We have already seen that students learn in many different ways, so this variety in the lesson gives all students a chance to make progress. As a result, students are often more motivated to pay attention and take part in the lesson.

EXTENDING YOUR COURSE BOOK

What do you do if your course book does not contain a wide selection of ways of learning? Why do we recommend that you should try to plan more variety?

Imagine that your students are preparing for an exam which tests their comprehension and grammar. Your course book has long texts and many repetitive grammar exercises. This will prepare them for the exam, but if the lessons always repeat the same format, they become monotonous, so your problem is keeping students (and yourself!) interested. It is good for both your students' motivation and your own motivation to introduce some different activities into the lesson.

You can try two strategies:

1. You can add activities that are not in your course book.
2. You can adapt activities that are already there.

You can use the activities and ideas in this book to help you. For example, the activities in Chapters 6 and 7 use vocabulary and grammar (to meet your students' need to learn this) but they also add variety to make your students more active and motivated. This will help them to learn better. The activities in this book will also give you ideas for adapting the activities in your course book. As you gain confidence, you can develop your own ideas.

In the next two chapters, we will look at how to organise lessons which include a variety of activities.

Classroom Action Task

Look at one of the books you use in class.

Does it focus on a grammatical or functional view of language or a mixture of these? (Use the examples earlier in this chapter as a reminder of how to do this.)

In your Teacher's Diary, write down the real needs of your students.

Do these match the view of language in the books you use in class?

4 / Organising Lessons to Teach New Language

In this chapter we look at a framework to organise English lessons to teach new words, grammar and functional language using a variety of teaching techniques and activities. In Chapter 5, we will look at a slightly different framework for lessons to practise language skills (reading, listening, writing and speaking).

These two chapters will give you simple and useful frameworks which you can use to plan one lesson or a whole series of lessons. Once you know these frameworks, you can build on them and adapt them by using the ideas and activities in this book, as well as your own ideas.

WHY IT IS IMPORTANT TO ORGANISE LESSONS

It is important to organise lessons well. As a teacher, you need to teach your syllabus and help your students learn well and succeed. You need to introduce new language, help students practise it and give students a chance to communicate freely with each other in English. You also want to make sure that you include a variety of teaching approaches in your lessons, to keep students motivated and to help them learn better.

So where do we start? Lessons that focus on using words, structures and functional language are taught in a slightly different way from lessons which improve students' reading, listening, writing and speaking skills. There are also many ways of organising the learning activities within a lesson. These depend on the level of your students and on how much English they hear and see outside school. All well-structured lessons have variety but they proceed in a logical way, so we need to start with the objectives of the lesson.

OBJECTIVES

When planning a lesson, you first have to decide on the objectives of the lesson. One way to set objectives is to think about what your students will know and be able to do at the end of the lesson, that they did not know or could not do at the beginning. Sometimes, these objectives are listed in your syllabus. A good course book usually has clear objectives set out in well-structured lessons.

Look at these detailed objectives:

Example A

By the end of the lesson, students will *know* and be able to *use* six verbs to describe daily routines, for example, wake up, brush teeth, get dressed, have breakfast, catch the bus, eat lunch.

The objective of this lesson is to teach students to use new vocabulary (words for daily routines).

Example B

By the end of the lesson, the students will *know* how to form and *ask* questions in the present tense, for example, 'Do you catch the eight o'clock bus every day?'.

The objective of this lesson is to teach students to use new grammar (how to form questions in the present tense).

Example C

By the end of the lesson, students will *know* and be able to *use* three ways to ask permission, for example, 'Can I . . . ?', 'Could I . . . ?', 'May I . . . ?'.

The objective of this lesson is to teach students to use a new language function (asking permission).

Example D

By the end of the lesson, students will be able to understand the main points of a news broadcast.

The objective of this lesson is for students to practise their listening skills (by listening to and understanding a news broadcast).

So you can see that we need to set objectives for all lessons, whether we are teaching a new language item (that is, vocabulary, grammar or functional language), or practising a language skill (reading, listening, writing and speaking).

LESSONS TO TEACH NEW LANGUAGE ITEMS (VOCABULARY, GRAMMAR AND FUNCTIONAL LANGUAGE)

First, we are going to look at a framework for a lesson which teaches new language items. It incorporates aspects of all the different teaching methods (some from the Grammar Translation teaching method, some from the Direct Methods and some from the Communicative Method). It is based on both a Grammatical and Functional view of language. This framework is called the PPP framework.

A PPP lesson is divided into three phases: Presentation, Practice and Production.

One of the best ways of helping students to reach the objectives of the lesson is to introduce the new language well in the first phase of the lesson: this is the Presentation phase. Then, students need to have plenty of activities to help them to practise the new language: this is the Practice phase. Lastly, the students need time to use the new language they have learned in order to communicate with each other: this is the Production phase.

At the beginning of a PPP lesson, only the teacher knows the new language item and how to use it. The teacher presents and teaches this language to the students by demonstrating it to them (modelling the language), explaining it and giving students lots of practice in how to use it. By the end of the lesson, during the Production phase, the new language becomes part of the students' own knowledge of language and they should be able to use it easily, together with other English that they have learned before.

This is a very useful framework because

- ▶ it is based on effective learning principles;
- ▶ it is an easy framework to use for planning a lesson or series of lessons;
- ▶ it ensures that students learn to use some language;
- ▶ the lesson is divided up into different activities or phases so that students are not bored;
- ▶ it has a good balance between teacher talking and student activity;
- ▶ it has a good balance of language skills;
- ▶ it includes all methods of language teaching;
- ▶ it is a flexible model and can be used for many different learning levels and contexts;

▶ it gives an opportunity for students to become more accurate in English;

▶ it gives an opportunity for students to practise becoming more fluent in English.

The PPP framework also

▶ provides a useful starting point for new teachers;

▶ aims to help students to understand and know about a new area of language;

▶ leads students to *use* this new language;

▶ encourages students to be more active in their learning;

▶ helps students to improve their speaking, writing, listening and reading.

So let's look at the phases of a PPP lesson in more detail. We have used examples of introducing new functional language to illustrate the lesson framework. You will find more activities for presenting new language items which you can use in PPP lessons in Chapters 6 to 8.

THE PRESENTATION PHASE

During the Presentation phase, the teacher introduces the new language items that the students need to learn. This new language may be some vocabulary, grammar, or functional language.

When presenting new language, the teacher must show three things very clearly:

1. What it means.
2. How and when it is used.
3. What it sounds like.

It is also important to show students how to form the vocabulary, grammar or functional language, and to check the spelling of new words.

Students need to understand the meaning of the new language, so the teacher must set the scene and put the new language into a very clear and obvious context. There are several ways of doing this:

1. The teacher uses real objects or pictures, or draws objects, people or a situation on the blackboard.
2. The teacher tells the students about a situation which demonstrates the meaning of the new language.
3. The students read a text or listen to a tape which contains examples of the new language. This can be a story or a dialogue.
4. The teacher mimes (acts without speaking) an action or emotion or acts out a role play or dialogue which helps show what the new language is and when it is used.

For example, to present the function of asking for something, 'Could you . . . ?', the teacher can act out a brief dialogue, as follows.

The teacher mimes that she does not have a pencil. Then she says the following dialogue (taking both parts):

Teacher A: 'I don't have a pencil. Could you lend me a pencil?'
Teacher B: 'Yes, of course.'

The teacher then checks that students understand when and how this function is used, by asking questions.

To make sure that you cover all the important information about a new language item in the Presentation stage, it is best to go through the following steps:

1. Set the scene using one of the techniques listed in points 1 to 4 above.
2. Model the new language, saying it two or three times.
3. Ask students to repeat the new language several times out loud, first the whole class, then in groups, then in pairs.
4. Ask questions to check that students understand the meaning of the new words, structure or function.
5. Write the new language item on the blackboard, marking in the stress and checking the spelling with the students.
6. If necessary, explain the grammar of the new language item.
7. Ask students to copy the information from the board into their notebooks.

Do not introduce new grammar and new vocabulary at the same time: this can be very confusing for students. If you introduce new grammar, it is important to check that the students already know the vocabulary of the scene or situation in which the grammar is presented. It is a good idea to check or, if necessary, to pre-teach this vocabulary before presenting new grammar. Similarly, when you introduce new vocabulary, present the new words in a grammatical structure which the students already know.

When you present new functional language, you do not need to explain the grammatical structure of the phrases. Encourage students to remember whole phrases and when they are used.

During the Presentation phase of the lesson, the teacher does most of the talking and has strong control over the students. The teacher expects students to write and to say the language very accurately. If they make mistakes in writing or speaking, the teacher corrects them.

You can see that by the end of the Presentation phase, the students understand the meaning of the new language, they can pronounce it correctly, they know how to spell it, and they understand the way it is formed. They have listened to it, repeated it, read it and written it down.

Now students need to practise the new language without so much support from the teacher.

THE PRACTICE PHASE

It is very important that students have enough practice of the new language. Students can do this by listening, repeating, writing and reading the new language, using a wide variety of learning activities. Students can practise individually, in pairs, in groups or as a whole class (see Chapter 18 for guidance on organising group and pair work).

Remember that practice must not begin until the teacher is sure that the students understand the language they are using. If the Presentation phase has been done well, this should not be a problem.

Practice should begin in a very simple way where the teacher controls everything the students say or write. At this stage, the teacher corrects sentence construction, use of the language, and pronunciation. We call this the Controlled Practice phase and it uses some of the repetition techniques used in the Direct Methods, such as drilling.

Drilling is a very controlled practice: it is the simplest way of practising. It can be rather mechanical and does not challenge the students to think, but it gives them the chance to physically practise pronouncing the new language, getting the sounds and intonation right and getting the words in the right order. This is why drilling is a very important technique of practising new language. There are more examples of written and spoken drills in Chapters 6 to 12.

For example, students can practise the new vocabulary, grammar or function by repeating sentences. The teacher says: 'I don't have a pencil. Could you lend me a pencil?', and the students repeat 'Could you lend me a pencil?'. The teacher says more similar phrases, and the students repeat the 'Could you . . . ?' phrase.

Later in the Practice phase, the students do activities with less teacher help and control. They must learn to practise the language in pairs; the teacher only guides the practice. We call these the less controlled or guided stages of the Practice phase. At these later stages the teacher should monitor. (To monitor means to check; for example, the teacher walks around the class listening and helping while students are doing practice activities individually or in pairs or groups.)

There are examples of less controlled activities for teaching vocabulary in Chapter 6, grammar in Chapter 7 and functional language in Chapter 8.

Most language lessons in school focus mainly on the presentation and practice of new language. At the end of these phases, students should be able to speak or write the new language fairly well without making many mistakes. So it is now time for the teacher to give students different activities which allow them to use the new language they have learned in a more free situation.

THE PRODUCTION PHASE

In the Production phase, students should do activities that they may have to do when they leave the classroom, for example, writing a letter or reading a newspaper article and telling someone about it, or taking part in an interview. We can think of this phase as the final rehearsal for using language in the real world.

Students should be encouraged to use other language they know or have already learned in previous lessons. During this part of the lesson, the teacher does not usually interrupt, help or correct errors. The students must learn to communicate successfully with only the help of their fellow students.

For example, as a Production activity for the functional language of asking someone to do something ('Could you . . . ?'), students act out a short dialogue between someone who has to get to school to write an exam. His bicycle has a puncture. He asks his friend 'Could you lend me your bicycle?' or 'Could you take me in your truck?' or 'Could you tell the teacher I will be late?'.

Table 4.1 summarises the different phases of a PPP lesson.

Table 4.1

	Presentation	Practice	Production
Teacher activity	Models and explains the meaning of new language items. Makes sure the students understand meaning, and know spelling, grammar and pronunciation.	Leads drilling. Organises guided and less controlled practice through speaking, listening, writing and reading.	Organises freer practice and fluency activities. Monitors students' activities and notes errors.
Student participation	Listens and understands meaning of new language items.	Repeats drills. Practises speaking, writing, reading and listening to new language items in pairs of groups.	Uses new language item and other known language in pairs or groups in freer practice and fluency activities.
Teacher control	Strongly in control, probably at the front of the class.	Strongly in control during drilling. Less visibly in control during guided practice.	Silently in control. May take control again for class correction after freer practice or fluency activities.
Correction	Teacher corrects all errors.	Teacher corrects and helps students correct all errors during drilling. Less obvious correction later in this phase.	Teacher notes errors but does not correct during the activities.

EXTENDING THE PPP FRAMEWORK

The PPP framework is very flexible. You can use it to plan a series of PPP lessons. You can also divide the phases and spend one whole lesson on each phase: for example, one whole lesson can be used for presenting a new language item, another lesson can be spent doing different kinds of Practice activities, and one or even several lessons can be spent doing Production activities. This extended version of the framework is very useful when lessons are only 30 or 40 minutes long and time can be lost taking the register or settling down. Students who already know a lot of English and need to practise their fluency need less controlled practice, but they can benefit from a longer production lesson.

The PPP framework, as we have seen, is useful for planning lessons which introduce new vocabulary, grammar or functional language.

During a PPP lesson, students use the four language skills of speaking, reading, writing and listening in order to practise the new language. So in a PPP lesson, you can include a focus on skills as well as the focus on new language. This way of building language skills into the lesson gives a variety of activities within a lesson, and the language-item and language-skills work reinforce each other.

However, you may want or need to give students time to focus only on improving their listening, speaking, reading and writing skills. In the next chapter, we look at how to organise a lesson to practise these language skills.

Classroom Action Task

Take a look at a lesson in your course book. Is it in any way based on a PPP framework?

Is there a variety of practice activities using all four language skills?

How could you include some practice activities in this lesson?

Are there any activities for free practice of the language (Production phase)?

Can you think of some free practice activities to build into this lesson?

5 / Organising Lessons to Improve Language Skills

In the previous chapter we looked at how to organise lessons to teach new language items. In this chapter we look at the background to the four language skills and show how to organise lessons which focus on improving students' reading, listening, speaking and writing skills.

Chapter 4 and this chapter give you simple and useful frameworks which you can use to plan one lesson or a whole series of lessons. Once you know these frameworks, you can build on them and adapt them by using the ideas and activities in this book, as well as your own ideas.

FEATURES OF LANGUAGE SKILLS

You will remember that some linguists divide language learning into the four language skills of listening, reading, speaking and writing. You may want to spend part or all of a lesson practising these skills. In order to practise these skills, students will usually not use new language, but will use language they already know. You do not need to introduce new language and this is why skills lessons are organised in a slightly different way from PPP lessons.

Let's first look at some of the features of reading, listening, speaking and writing which helps us, as teachers, understand better how our students learn these skills. Then we can see how to organise a lesson and plan activities to help students practise the skills.

Reading and listening have some similar features. When students read and listen to English, they only have to *recognise* and *understand* the language that they read or listen to. So we call these the two 'receptive' skills. Speaking and writing also have some similar features. When students speak or write, they have to *produce* language. So we call these the 'productive' skills.

Reading also has some features which are similar to writing. When students read or write, they have time to think about the meaning of the language. They can read the text again, they can rewrite and correct what they have written. They have time to think about what they have read or written.

When students listen or speak, they have less time: they have to react quickly. In real-life situations, you usually only hear something once. Sometimes you can ask someone to repeat it – but you cannot do that if you are listening to a station announcement or to the television or radio. When someone asks you a question, you have to understand what they said, think of a reply and say it in English – in a short space of time.

These different features of reading, listening, speaking and writing mean that we need to plan our lessons to give students different kinds of learning activities to practise each language skill.

Speaking and writing can be taught and practised either as part of a PPP lesson or as a separate lesson. So first, let's look at a slightly different lesson framework for teaching reading and listening.

A LANGUAGE SKILLS LESSON FOR TEACHING READING AND LISTENING

We plan a reading skills or listening skills lesson in three parts:

1. Before-reading, or before-listening activities.
2. During-reading, or during-listening activities.
3. After-reading, or after-listening activities.

These phases reflect what we do in real life when we read or listen. Think about how we read and listen in our own language. We usually read or listen for a reason: we may do it for pleasure or to get information. We also usually choose to read or to listen. We may read a newspaper or a letter from a friend. We may listen to a weekly sports programme on the radio or to an announcement at the railway or bus station.

So, before we read or listen in our own language, we usually already know something about the text we are reading, or what we are listening to. We know the kind of language which will probably be used. We can often predict what some of the information will be, based upon our previous knowledge or interest in the subject. For example, if we are listening to a radio sports programme, we expect to hear the names of athletes, players and teams. The information we choose to read or listen to is not often completely new or uninteresting to us. This is a skill called *prediction*.

In the 'Before' phase, students prepare for the main reading or listening activity. The purpose of 'before-reading' or 'before-listening' activities is to help students to think about the activity and to motivate them to read the text, or listen to the story or conversation. The activities aim to help students use the skill of prediction: to predict what kind of language that they will see or read, and to predict some of the content.

Then, while we read or listen in our own language, we usually do this in two ways. We may want to find out the general idea or topic of something we are reading or listening to, or we may want some very specific information. To find a general idea, we read or listen to everything from start to end, so that we can identify the main idea. This sub-skill is called reading or listening *for the main idea(s)*. If we want very specific information from what we are reading or from the person we are listening to, then we try to select the particular information we want: we do not worry about other information or ideas that we do not need. This sub-skill is called reading or listening *for specific information*.

In the 'During' phase, the teacher gives the students a task to do while they are reading or listening. The purpose of the task is to give students a real reason to read or listen. The teacher can set different types of tasks in order to help students to read or listen either for the general idea or for specific information.

Finally, in real life, we usually take action after we have read something or listened to something. We reply, we tell a friend about it, we make a note of it, we write to someone about it, or we act upon it (we catch the right train or bus!).

In the 'After' phase of the lesson, it is useful to do activities which require students to react to what they have read or listened to by using the information they have found out. This allows you to check whether your students have understood what they have read or what they have listened to, and to practise reading and listening in real-life situations.

This means that when we organise a reading or listening lesson, we need to give students practice in

- ▶ predicting what type of information might be in the text or listening activity;
- ▶ reading a whole text or listening to a whole item and finding some general information about it;
- ▶ reading or listening for some specific information;
- ▶ using the context to guess unknown words in a text or listening activity;
- ▶ recording, discussing or acting on what they have heard or read.

Students who are good at these skills will find that their reading and listening improves, which makes them more motivated.

We have said that in a 'Before–During–After' lesson, you may need to include PPP elements (such as presenting new vocabulary). Here is an example of a lesson plan for a 'Before–During–After' lesson which includes these elements:

A 'Before–During–After' language skills lesson, with PPP activities

Objective: students practise reading a story for the main ideas.

Before-reading activity
Discuss the title (for example, 'A disastrous adventure'). Students suggest words connected to the topic which may appear in the text, and possible story lines (without reading the story).

[*New vocabulary* – optional PPP activity: present and teach key words from the text to make sure that students understand the meaning, the use and the correct pronunciation of the new words.]

During-reading activity
Students read the story within a time limit to encourage faster reading, and fill in a chart to note what happened, and when.

After-reading activity
Students compare their charts (without the text in front of them) in pairs or groups to confirm what they read. Then students individually write a letter to a friend about the incident.

[*Functional language* – optional PPP activity: to practise the 3rd conditional using information from the story, for example: 'If he hadn't left home late, he wouldn't have missed the bus.' Students suggest further examples and then the teacher checks the meaning of the 3rd conditional. Students work through the events in the story by drilling and controlled pair work.]

TEACHING SPEAKING AND WRITING SKILLS

We have seen how a lesson or part of a lesson to improve reading or listening is divided into 'before', 'during' and 'after' phases. If we want to spend a whole lesson practising speaking and writing, we use the PPP framework we looked at in Chapter 4, but in a slightly different way. Let's look at why this is.

You may remember that we call speaking and writing 'productive' skills. This is because students have to actively produce language in order to speak and write. They have to remember and use language which they already know, and produce a spoken sentence or dialogue, or write a text.

This can be a challenge. Students are sometimes unwilling or shy about speaking English in class or about having a conversation in English. If students in your country do not need to speak English outside the classroom, it can be a real challenge to motivate them to say anything in English.

Writing involves all aspects of language: grammar, vocabulary, word order, spelling and logical arrangement of ideas. Students often make mistakes when they start to write in sentences. This means that the teacher has a lot of marking to do, and all the corrections in red pen do not make the students very happy. They also do not help the students very much.

This is why we need to plan lessons or parts of lessons which progress in a step-by-step way. They start with guided and controlled activities and move towards less-guided and more student-centred and creative activities. Guided activities which are easy and short will help all students to speak or write with few mistakes in a controlled situation. As their confidence and interest grow, less-guided activities will encourage them to speak and write more confidently. They will make fewer mistakes and can become more confident and creative in speaking and writing.

So here are the outline lesson stages of a speaking or writing lesson:

1. Present or revise the language that the students will need in a controlled situation. Remember: do not teach new structures and new vocabulary in the same lesson.
2. Give students practice with the language they will need, moving from controlled practice (this can include drilling or written controlled practice) to guided practice.
3. Let students have freer practice in pairs or groups, to personalise and practise producing language fluently or doing extended writing.

As you can see, the controlled to less-guided phases (1 and 2 above) are part of the PPP framework (look back to Chapter 4): in the Practice phase, the class first does very controlled exercises. Then, the lesson moves to less controlled activities, and finally, in the Production phase, students do activities on their own with very little help from the teacher.

However, remember that during a PPP lesson which teaches vocabulary, grammar and functional language (see Chapter 4), students are using the language skills in order to practise new language. This means that the main focus of the lesson is not on practising the skill, but on learning a new language item (in the example in Chapter 4, we used the function of asking someone to do something, 'Could you . . . ?').

So, when you are planning a lesson or part of a lesson where the focus is only on improving and practising speaking or writing, the Presentation and guided Practice phases should be shorter and lead quickly on to the main part of the lesson (the Production phase), when the focus is on producing spoken or written language with fluency and creativity.

Here is a lesson plan which shows how language skills activities are included in a PPP framework.

Lesson for presenting new grammar, with activities for improving language skills

Objective
By the end of the lesson, students will be able to use the present continuous to describe present action.

Example of target language:
'What's she doing?' 'She's writing on the blackboard.'

Presentation phase
Explain new language with action pictures, then check meaning, use and pronunciation.

Practice phase
Class drills, using word prompts and then picture word prompts.

[*Optional skills improvement activity* – The teacher asks students to make sentences which they would hear in a sports commentary of a race or a football match. The students work in pairs to write two sentences and then each pair reads out their sentences. The teacher writes the sentences on the blackboard. More advanced students can be asked to suggest sentences, without writing them down first. The teacher then writes these on the blackboard.]

Production phase (the main part of the lesson)
In pairs or groups, students mime various activities and the others have to guess what they are doing.

[*Optional skills improvement activity* – Act out a mobile phone call, telling someone what you are doing while you are walking around and talking to them. For example: 'I'm walking out of the room, and now I'm going upstairs. Now I'm looking out of the window.']

We have now looked at some simple techniques which you can use to plan lessons to teach all the aspects of your syllabus. We have also looked at some examples of how we can use these techniques to include a variety of teaching activities, which will help our students to learn to use English better.

Chapters 6 to 12 contain ideas and activities for teaching language items and language skills which have been developed by English teachers from all over the world, including Bangladesh, People's Republic of Congo, China, Cameroon, Eritrea, Ghana, Nepal, Nigeria, Pakistan and St Vincent.

6 / Ideas for Teaching Vocabulary

This chapter contains activities for teaching vocabulary within the PPP lesson framework. There is a variety of practical and helpful classroom activities to practise, record and store new vocabulary. If you have a large class and few or no resources, many of these activities are a good way of encouraging group activities and learning how to make class resources co-operatively.

IDEAS FOR TEACHING VOCABULARY

Students learn new vocabulary in two stages. First, when they read or hear new words, they know about the word and can usually recognise it, but they are not yet ready to use it in speech or writing. Later, when they start to use the word, it becomes part of their active vocabulary. However, this process of learning to use new words can take a long time. Usually, common and useful everyday words become our active vocabulary first. To speed up this process, we can help students by providing useful ideas for recording and storing new words and giving lots of practice with new words.

Here is a summary of important points to remember about presenting practising, recording and storing vocabulary:

► When presenting new vocabulary, you must teach its meaning and pronunciation.
► The precise meaning of new words, in specific contexts, is very important.
► The meaning of new words can be taught through pictures, mime, real objects, as well as from a situation in context.
► Teachers need to ask questions to check that students understand the meaning.
► Students need lots of varied practice of new vocabulary.
► Students need to revise new vocabulary regularly.
► Students need to record and store new vocabulary in a helpful way. Well-recorded new vocabulary can improve students' learning.

PRESENTATION PHASE

When we present new vocabulary, we need to teach students what the word means, its pronunciation and how to use the word. For example, the teacher demonstrates the meaning of a word or phrase by showing a picture or real object, or by doing an action. When the teacher has checked that the students understand, she repeats the phrase and the students then repeat it chorally (all together) or in pairs or groups until they can say it perfectly. Then the teacher demonstrates another word or shows another picture and the students repeat a slightly different response.

The teacher can present new words in a dialogue, taking both parts, first standing in one place to speak as one character and then moving to speak as the other character. For younger students, using puppets as characters is another good way to demonstrate the meaning of new language. However, all vocabulary needs to be presented quickly and effectively, so that students can practise using the new words as quickly as possible.

PRACTICE PHASE

Remember that students need lots of practice with new vocabulary in order to remember and use the new words. If you use different kinds of practice activities then you and your students can benefit from the variety. Here are some ideas.

Practising new vocabulary

Students can enjoy practising new vocabulary through a large variety of word games. These are either specially made up for language students or adapted from well-known games that people play in different parts of the world.

Dominoes

Students can play different matching games with domino-like cards; for example, they can match words and pictures, or match the word in their first language to the word in English, or match words to their definitions.

At lower levels, you can use single words and at higher levels you can use phrasal verbs or idioms. (For example, the phrasal verb 'to get out of' can be matched with the equivalent single-word verb 'to escape'.)

The whole class can help to make the domino cards as a learning activity in itself. The class, however large, is divided into groups, and each group makes a set of cards. First, the teacher and the class choose a set of words, which the teacher writes on the blackboard. Each student is given two or three pieces of card, such as cut-up cardboard packaging. Each student then writes a word from a set of words chosen by the teacher and the class, and draws a simple drawing (for nouns such as 'dog', 'tree' or 'moon') on each piece of card. The complete set of cards can be matched up and played like the matching of the sets of spots on dominoes (see Figure 6.1).

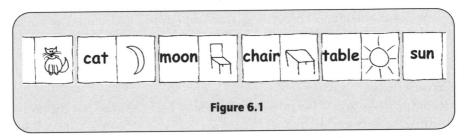

Figure 6.1

Bingo

The class can make sets of bingo cards by cutting up used packaging. Make sets of cards, one for each student. Each card has between six and twelve words written on it, chosen randomly from a selection of new words which students need to practise. It is useful to include words learned several weeks before, as well as recently learned words.

Give each student or group a card. Then you or a student reads out the complete list of words, one by one. If a student or group thinks that they have that word on their card, they cross it off (if the cards will be used again, students can also write the word down on a separate piece of paper or place a stone on the word). The winner is the first person or group who has crossed off all their words (Figure 6.2).

cat	moon	like
blue	carrot	live
chair	my	table
happy	our	sun

Figure 6.2

Spelling activities on the blackboard

► Putting the jumbled-up letters of known words into the correct order.

► Making short words out of longer words.

► Guessing the word from the correct number of blank spaces, letter by letter.

► Noughts and crosses: play this game as individuals or in small groups. Draw a grid on the blackboard, on sheets of paper or on the ground outside. A correctly spelt word entitles the winner to place a 0 or an X (or different types of stones) on the grid. The winner is the person or group that completes a row of noughts or crosses first.

Crosswords

Students make and solve crosswords, where half the class, or different groups, think of and write half the clues (the 'up' or 'down' clues). The different groups then swap with another group and fill in their half of the crossword.

Alphabet lists

Pick a letter and fill in a word for each given category, for example, colours, animals, flowers, fruit, vegetables, etc. This can be done as an individual or group competition. The winner is, for example, the first to fill in twenty words, or the group or student who fills in the most words in five minutes (Figure 6.3).

	Colour	Animal	Fruit	Vegetable
A			apple	
B	blue		banana	
C	cream	cat		carrot
D		dog		
E		elephant		

Figure 6.3

Memorising lists

Go round the group or class, in random order. The first student thinks of an item from a list, for example, a shopping list or a list of favourite games. The next student repeats the word and adds their own word. The other students, in turn, repeat the full list and each student adds an item of his or her own. The list gets longer and more difficult to remember.

Simple 'Scrabble'

You can play this crossword game on the blackboard with the class as individuals, or in small groups, each with their own board. You and your students can easily make your own 'Scrabble' sets for classroom use:

1. Draw a frame of fifteen by fifteen squares on the blackboard; or each group can draw their own frame on a piece of paper or card.
2. Cut out small squares which fit onto the board squares, making enough for about ten to fifteen for each student in the class.
3. Draw one letter of the alphabet onto each of the small squares, making twice as many vowels as consonants.
4. Give each student or each group a random set of about six to eight letters. Place the remaining letters face down.
5. Playing in turn, each student or group tries to make a complete word from their letters, or to add letters to form a complete word, by writing the word on the blackboard or by placing the word on the frame.
6. Replace the letters that they used by taking the same number of letters.
7. If a person or group cannot make a word, they lose their turn.

The end of the game of Simple 'Scrabble' is when a person or group finishes all their letters.

You can add other activities based on similar learning games.

Recording and storing new vocabulary

Students need to record and store new vocabulary in a logical and helpful way, so that they can find old words and they can add new words easily and quickly. Language students have different ways of doing this, and a common way is to name a page or two for each letter of the alphabet and then add words under their first letter. However, recording words in this way means that it is not always easy to find the words you want. If you cannot remember what letter of the alphabet the word you want starts with, it can be difficult!

Prefixes and suffixes

If students know the word 'happy', they can make and understand at least five new but connected words by adding the prefix and suffixes: 'un-', '-ily', '-ness', '-ier' or '-iest'. A visual way of recording these sets of words is in a bubble diagram (Figure 6.4).

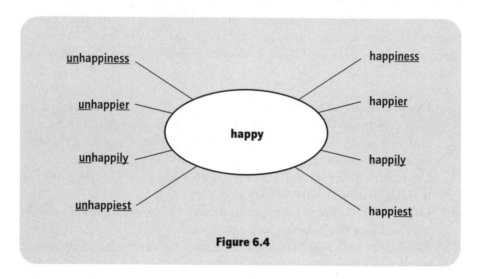

Figure 6.4

Head words

Students can record head words (sets of words with the same general meaning) together. For example: 'ways of speaking' or 'ways of walking'. Also, it is helpful to record words which are connected, directly or indirectly, to a head word, such as 'kitchen'. Recording these in the form of a bubble diagram instead of a list is also useful (Figure 6.5).

Word cards

A different and useful way of storing and recording new words is for students to make and use personal pocket word cards. One way of helping students with this additional activity is to help them write their own cards, in the minutes sometimes left at the end of the day or at the end of the week. Ask your class to cut out small cards (about 5cm × 2.5cm) from bits of scrap paper or card from used packaging. Then, everyone chooses the words they want to learn, from about five to ten words. On one side of the card, the word is written in English and on the

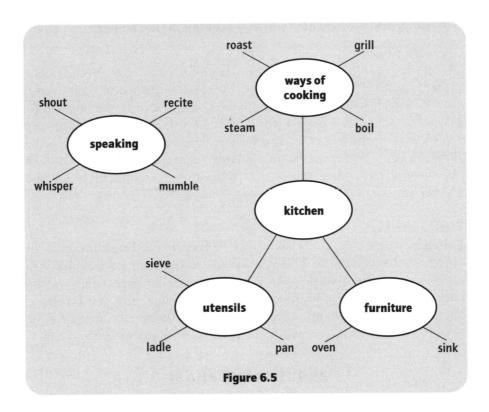

Figure 6.5

other side of the card is the word in the student's first or main tongue, or/and a picture, a sentence using the word, the grammar of the word, its pronunciation, and any synonyms (Figure 6.6).

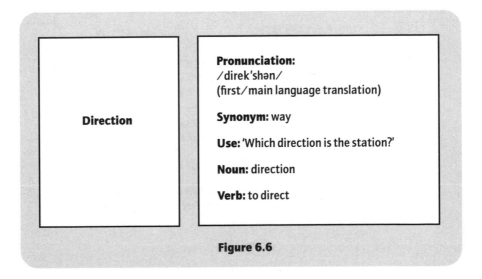

Figure 6.6

Recording and storing new words – whole-class activities

Class dictionary

The pocket card idea can easily be adapted for class use. You or your students make a class dictionary box for revision games and self-study, classified in alphabetical order or by topic. The cards in the box can be a larger version of the pocket word cards, and they can be stored in any box or used packaging of a suitable size. The sets of words can also be stored in cloth pockets sewn onto a large square of old fabric. You can place these class dictionaries in an easily accessible place in the classroom.

Class labelling

Labelling is an easy and visible way to record the English names of objects in the classroom. This helps students by linking a real object to the written word. You or your students can make large labels on the back of used paper or from card packaging. Then stick the labels on objects in your classroom. Like the classroom dictionary, these can be used for class learning games or for self-study look-and-learn.

PRODUCTION PHASE

Production activities for new vocabulary will usually be part of the Production phase of a speaking or writing skills lesson, or a grammar or functional language lesson (Figure 6.7).

Language that has been taught	Production activity
Adjectives to describe people	A letter to a new friend from another town telling her how to spot you at the bus stop
Words about houses	Students write an article for their school magazine about their dream house
Words about ways of travelling	Students discuss an imaginary journey the class is planning

Figure 6.7

Classroom Action Task

Start students making a class dictionary and encourage students to study the class dictionary if they finish work early.

Plan revision games regularly, using words learned during the term.

Also encourage students to make and use their own small pocket dictionary cards.

7 / Ideas for Teaching Grammar

You may be a teacher who normally teaches students to understand and translate texts by studying the vocabulary and grammar in your own language. In other words, you use a Grammar Translation method to teach English. The activities in this chapter will introduce some variety into your lessons, while giving your students a good knowledge of grammar in order to prepare for their exams.

First, let's have a brief look at how all teachers, whether new or experienced, can improve their own knowledge of grammar. Then we shall look at activities which present grammatical structures to our students in a clear and interesting way, and which help to practise using these structures correctly.

IMPROVING YOUR OWN KNOWLEDGE OF GRAMMAR

There are many ways in which you can revise and improve your own English grammar. You can learn on the job. Don't expect to learn the whole of English grammar before you teach it, but spend time reading and studying the structure you are going to teach when you plan your next lesson. Try to find a grammar book that you find easy to understand, or find someone (maybe another teacher) who will help you. Make notes on the grammar you need for the next lesson in a way that you understand. Keep your notes carefully. If you do this during the year as you teach, then at the end of the year, you will have your own grammar book which is completely relevant for your own teaching and which you can easily understand.

Let's think about the sort of information you might want to record about a grammatical structure, for example, the present tense (Figure 7.1).

You may also need to know the names of all the tenses, together with an example, so you can make a diagram like that shown in Figure 7.2.

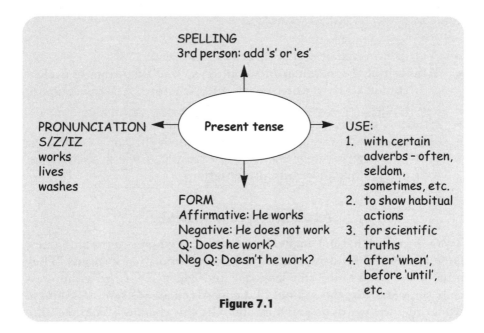

SPELLING
3rd person: add 's' or 'es'

PRONUNCIATION
S/Z/IZ
works
lives
washes

Present tense

USE:
1. with certain adverbs – often, seldom, sometimes, etc.
2. to show habitual actions
3. for scientific truths
4. after 'when', before 'until', etc.

FORM
Affirmative: He works
Negative: He does not work
Q: Does he work?
Neg Q: Doesn't he work?

Figure 7.1

	SIMPLE	CONTINUOUS or PROGRESSIVE
Present	He works	He is working
Past	He worked	He was working
Present perfect	He has worked	He has been working
Past perfect	He had worked	He had been working
Future	He will work	He will be working
Future perfect	He will have worked	He will have been working

Figure 7.2

However, *using* grammar is just as important as *knowing about* grammar. By using the PPP framework for planning lessons, you will help students to apply their knowledge. Here are some activities for presenting and practising grammar. You can adapt the activities to practise the structures that are in your course book or ones that your students need to study for the exams.

When teaching grammar remember:

▶ You can present grammar directly or indirectly.
▶ Always put the grammar in a context so that the meaning is clear and students know when to use the structure. Ask questions to check this.
▶ Students need to practise the new grammar.
▶ There is a wide variety of activities in which students can practise using the new grammar fluently; for example, discussions, debates, role plays, simulations and presentations.

PRESENTATION PHASE

You remember that in Chapter 4, we saw that when you present a new language item to students, they must understand what it means. They must know *when* to use this language and *how* it is formed grammatically (how and why the endings of the words change (Example 1) and in what order the words go and how and why this changes (Example 2).

Example 1: I play the violin: You play the violin: He plays the violin:
Example 2: He can play the guitar.
      (Question form): Can he play the guitar?

There are several ways of presenting new grammar to students. 'Overt', or direct, teaching of grammar is when the teacher presents the grammatical rules and information. 'Covert', or indirect, teaching of grammar is when the teacher does not explain the grammar to the students, but helps them to understand it in different ways. Let's look at how we can use these approaches.

Presenting language directly

In this approach, the teacher clearly presents rules and explanations. For example, to teach the question form in Example 2 above, the teacher tells the students that to make questions in the present tense using 'Can', you must invert the subject of the sentence and the modal auxiliary. This inversion is then followed by the bare infinitive of the verb 'to play' – the infinite without 'to'.

The teacher can then give other examples to help students understand the meaning of the new language, so that they know that you use 'Can you . . . ?' or 'Can he . . . ?' to ask about someone's ability to do something. The teacher can also draw a clear diagram on the blackboard to help students understand the grammar. (In Chapter 19 there are more ideas for using the blackboard to present grammar.)

Presenting grammar through a text

Another way of presenting grammar directly is by asking the students to underline particular grammatical points in the text. Students then have to work out a grammatical rule. They can do this by discussion in pairs or groups.

Example: underline all the examples of the past tense in these sentences. How do you think the past tense is formed?

'Yesterday, I worked in the fields until dusk. As the sun faded, I leaned against the old tree and looked with pride at the neat rows of seedlings. Then I gathered up my tools and walked towards the house.'

This technique can be used with many grammatical structures like conditionals, conjunctions, comparatives, pronouns, adjectives, etc.

Presenting grammar through comparison

The teacher puts two similar grammatical structures on the board. Students must discuss the differences in form, meaning and use.

Example: 'My sister lived in Kampala for three years.'
　　　　　'My sister has lived in Kampala for three years.'

This technique is particularly useful when comparing the different uses of tenses. (The timeline, Figure 7.4, can help present these structures.)

Presenting grammar indirectly

In this approach, the teacher does not draw the students' attention to any specific grammatical information. Let's look at some examples of how we can do this.

Presenting through a situation

The teacher either tells a simple anecdote or story or draws a series of pictures which give an outline of a situation.

Grammatical structure: He should have . . . /He shouldn't have . . .

Example:
Teacher: 'Last week a friend came from England. He was very tired after his flight. It was very hot and sunny. At 10 in the morning, my friend put on his swimsuit and sat in the garden reading his book. After

a half an hour he went to sleep. The sun came out and the temperature was 35°C. At two o'clock, he woke up. He was badly burnt and felt very sick. When we put him to bed he was shivering and feverish. What did he do wrong?'

Sometimes, one or two students will already know the right phrase, but if they do not know it the teacher has to tell them. 'He should have worn a shirt.' Students should then be able to think of other things the friend *should* or *shouldn't have* done in order to practise using the phrases. The teacher must check that students understand the meaning by asking questions like 'What is your advice to him?', 'Did he have to sit in the garden?', 'Did he know he would burn?', etc.

Presenting grammar through pictures and real objects
Grammatical structure: prepositions of place ('on', 'in', 'between', 'under').

The teacher draws a room on the blackboard or shows students a large picture of a room. He now asks questions about the position of things in the room. 'Where is the radio?' Once again, some students may know the new language already and can supply the prepositions: 'It is on the table.' If none of them knows it, the teacher must say the sentence clearly and teach the prepositions. You can also use real objects or your students to do this kind of presentation.

Using the students' knowledge to present grammar
Grammatical structure: comparison of adjectives: . . . er than . . .

Teacher asks: 'Is Guiyang big or small?'
Students reply: 'Big'
Teacher says: 'Yes, it is big, but Beijing is very big. It is bigger than Guiyang.'
Students reply: 'Bejing is bigger than Guiyang.'

Then the teacher can then write the populations of Beijing and Guiyang on the blackboard in two columns like this:

Beijing	*Guiyang*
12 million	2 million

Presenting a grammatical structure indirectly is often an easy way to make students understand the meaning and when to use the structure. Many teachers then go on to openly explain the grammatical form and teach the pronunciation and the spelling.

Using diagrams and time lines to help students understand grammar

It is sometimes easier for students to understand the meaning of a grammatical structure by looking at a diagram. Clear blackboard presentation is very important. You can use boxes, underlining and arrows to show the relationship of words in a sentence (Figure 7.3).

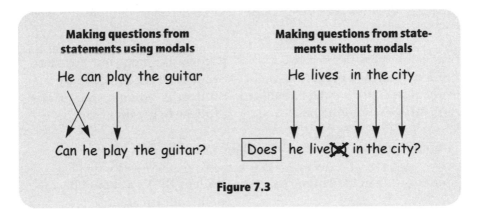

Figure 7.3

Time lines are a very good way of showing lengths of time and their relation to present time (Figure 7.4).

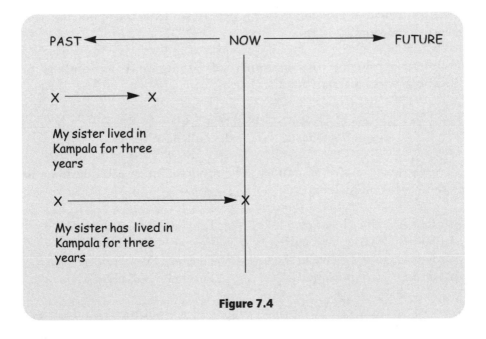

Figure 7.4

PRACTICE PHASE

Once students understand a new grammatical structure, they need a chance to practise it by drilling, writing, reading and listening.

Example: 'should have', shouldn't have'.

Students practise speaking in pairs from a series of cues on the board such as

Student A: Very hungry.   Student B: eaten your breakfast.
Student A: Really tired.   Student B: gone to bed earlier.
Student A: Can't see the blackboard. Student B: brought your glasses.
Student A: Missed the bus.   Student B: got up in time.

Students practise dialogues from these cues like this:

Student A: 'I'm very hungry.'   Student B: 'You should have
                                   eaten your breakfast.'

Controlled written grammar exercises are useful and can be done as homework, for example, changing all verbs in a text into the past tense, changing all sentences from 1st to 3rd person.

Less controlled or guided practice will give students the opportunity to use the new language item.

Example: practising the grammar of asking and responding to questions with different auxiliary verbs.

Language: Does it . . ./Has it . . ./Is it . . . ?
          Yes, it does/has/is. No, it doesn't/hasn't/isn't.

The teacher thinks of an animal. The students must ask questions to find out what animal it is.

Student A: 'Does it eat people?'   Teacher: 'No, it doesn't.'
Student B: 'Has it got a tail?'   Teacher: 'Yes, it has.'
Student C: 'Does it live in the forest?' Teacher: 'Yes, it does.'
Student D: 'Is it poisonous?'   Teacher: 'No, it isn't.'

Now the activity can be repeated in groups so that many students get the chance to ask and answer questions.

PRODUCTION PHASE

In the Presentation and Practice phases, the teacher normally uses prepared sentences or texts which contain the grammatical structure. When you start the Production phase of the lesson, it is a good idea to change the context of the presentation and the practice and to use activities based on students' own lives.

For example, using the grammar we used above of 'should have' and 'shouldn't have', each student in a group can think of something difficult or unpleasant that happened to them. Others in the group can then tell them what they should or should not have done. Students can write about what they did at certain ages (when they were 6 or 10 or 13) to practise regular or irregular verbs in the past tense.

Production activities which are related to the lives of students allow them to express their own opinions and ideas on a text or items from the coursebook. These kinds of activities are motivating and interesting.

Classroom Action Task

Choose a grammatical structure that you are going to teach your students soon.

Make sure you understand the meaning and that you know the form, and how and when this structure is used.

Think of a situation in which you might use this grammatical structure. Either practise telling the story or draw a series of pictures which tell the story. Now you are ready to present this grammar.

Decide how you can present this clearly on the board (look at Chapter 19).

Think of a series of cues which will prompt your students to practise this structure.

When you have taught the lesson, don't forget to make notes about how the lesson went. Then discuss the lesson with your colleagues and see if you should make any changes.

8 / Ideas for Teaching Functional Language

PRESENTATION PHASE

A good way of presenting functional language is using mime or acting. Puppets are useful for younger students.

Example: new language – the function of asking someone to do something ('Could you . . . ?').

1. The teacher starts by miming (acting without speaking) that she does not have a pencil. She searches on her desk, in her bag and in her pockets. The teacher can then act both speakers in the dialogue:

Teacher (as Teacher A) says: 'Could you lend me a pencil?'
Teacher (as Teacher B) says: 'Yes, of course.' (Mimes giving Teacher A a pencil.)

2. The teacher now gives the correct pronunciation and intonation pattern of these phrases, repeating them two or three times (see Chapter 18).

The teacher then repeats Steps 1 and 2 using different actions. For example, the teacher carries a big pile of books or a heavy box towards a closed door and says:

Teacher (as Teacher A) says: 'Could you open the door?'
Teacher (as Teacher B) says: 'Yes, of course.' (Opens the door.)

After each demonstration, the students do drilling by repeating the phrases two or three times: first the whole class, then half the class taking one part of the dialogue and the other half responding. The teacher corrects the phrase and the pronunciation.

The teacher then asks the students questions to check whether they understand the meaning and use of the phrases.

T:	'Have I got a pencil?'	Ss:	No
T:	(Indicating Teacher B) 'Has he got a pencil?'	Ss:	Yes
T:	(As Teacher A) 'Do I want to write?'	Ss:	Yes
T:	(As Teacher A) 'Do I want him to give me his pencil?'	Ss:	Yes

or

T:	'Is the door closed?'	Ss:	Yes
T:	'Are the books very heavy?'	Ss:	Yes
T:	'Is it possible for me to open the door?'	Ss:	No
T:	'Does he have any heavy books?'	Ss:	No
T:	Is it possible/easy for him to open the door?	Ss:	Yes
T:	'Do I want him to open the door?'	Ss:	Yes

The teacher can check in the students' first language that they understand the idea that 'Could you . . . ' is used to ask someone to do something for you.

The teacher writes the original dialogue on the blackboard, leaving out some of the words. Students read the dialogue, remembering the words that are missing. The teacher or a student can write these on the blackboard. The whole class can help to check that this is correct.

(Remember that when presenting a function, the teacher does not need to explain the grammatical structure of the phrases. Students should try to remember whole phrases and understand when to use them.)

The students copy the dialogue from the board into their books.

PRACTICE PHASE

Controlled speaking practice and drilling

As we saw in Chapter 4, drilling is a very useful way of practising new language.

The whole class can practise the new language by drilling, that is, speaking together at the same time (this is called choral practice). Students can also do choral practice in rows, groups or pairs. Remember that, in Chapter 5, we said that it can be a challenge to motivate students to speak English. Choral practice gives all students time to practise without having to say anything alone in front of the whole class, and builds their confidence.

When you start drilling, say the new language several times so students can repeat the language accurately. Make sure that:

1. they all speak together;
2. they all speak at normal speed;
3. they all imitate the sounds and intonation correctly.

Use your hands to 'conduct', as in Figure 8.1, in order to start all students speaking at the same time. You can also show the intonation and stress of the language with the hands (see Chapter 18).

Figure 8.1

The teacher can use different prompts or cues to encourage students to respond. These may be real objects, or objects shown on the black-board, or cue cards (cards with words or pictures that everyone can see) that the teacher holds up for the class to see.

Example: practising the function of talking about likes and dislikes and responding.

Language: 'Do you like . . . ?'. 'Yes, I do/No, I don't.'

Teacher (showing a picture of some oranges) says:
'Do you like oranges?'
Students repeat: 'Do you like oranges?'

Teacher (playing the part of another person) says:
'Yes, I do.'
Students repeat: 'Yes, I do.'

Teachers (showing a picture of some bananas) says:
'Do you like bananas?'
Students repeat: 'Do you like bananas?'

Teacher (playing the part of another person) says:
'No, I don't.'

The whole class repeats the word or phrase several times. For dialogues, you can divide the class in two, and let each half take the part of one person in the dialogue, speaking in chorus. Then, choose two confident students to say the dialogue to the class (open pairs). Finally, you demonstrate with one student (always choose a confident one first) and then tell all students to practise in pairs in the same way (closed pairs). This kind of drilling should not take more than a few minutes.

Less controlled speaking practice

A substitution table is a way of giving students further practice with less teacher control while making sure they do not make mistakes. The teacher writes a sentence or parts of a dialogue on the blackboard, putting parts that can be substituted into different columns. The students choose the correct words from each column to make a correct sentence or dialogue. They can then practise the questions and answers in pairs, working through all the alternatives (Figure 8.2).

Example: practising the function of inviting and responding.
Language: 'Would you like ...?'. 'No, I'd rather ...'.

Would you like to	play	football?
	go to	a café?
	watch	a match?
No, I'd rather	see	a film
		the festival

Figure 8.2

This practice can also be done in groups. Each member of the group has a card with one of the activities marked on it (e.g., 'Go to the festival'). The student must invite another student to do the activity on the card with him.

Student A: 'Would you like to go to the festival?'
Student B: 'No, I'd rather play football.'
              (to another student) 'Would you like to play football?'
Student C: 'No, I'd rather watch television.'
              (to another student) 'Would you like to watch television?'
              (Figure 8.3.)

Figure 8.3

Meaningful or communicative drills

Most drills are a repetition of the language item that the students have just learned. In classes where students have a wider vocabulary, you can make drilling more realistic – students can add their own ideas. For example, in the drill above, after practising the language item or dialogue to get that correct, students can add their own ideas, likes and dislikes and other information from their own lives. We call this the 'personalisation' of new language. Students usually find this kind of practice very motivating.

Even when the students' use of language is more limited, the teacher can set up more meaningful drills by giving students a choice of responses. For example, the teacher lists or draws eight or ten vegetables on the blackboard. Students choose four and copy them or write them down without showing anyone else. Then they practise in pairs:

Example: practising the function of asking for and giving information.

Language: 'Have you got any . . . ?'. 'Yes, I have/No, sorry, I haven't'.

Student A   (choosing an item from his list): 'Have you got any
             potatoes?'
Student B   (looking at her list of chosen items): 'No, sorry, I haven't.'
Student A   (choosing another item from his list): 'Have you got any
             white beans?'
Student B   (looking at her list): 'Yes, I have.'

This kind of activity, where one student has to find out some information that she or he does not know from another student, is called an 'information gap' activity (see Chapters 19 and 20 for information gap activities with limited resources).

Guided speaking practice

Guided practice comes at the end of the Practice phase of the lesson, when students have already had plenty of controlled practice. You can organise some guided practice if they already know enough English to carry out a conversation and simply need something to talk about. Guided practice will give them the opportunity to use the new language item. (Remember that drilling can also be used to practise grammatical structures.)

PRODUCTION PHASE

By now students have had plenty of practice using the new functional language so the activities in the production phase should encourage them to use the language without teacher control. It is a good idea to set activities which are related to real-life situations. An example is shown in Figure 8.4.

Language that has been taught	Production activity
Function of complaining	A role play in pairs. One student is a shopkeeper, the other is a customer who has bought something which does not work.

Figure 8.4

9 / Ideas for Improving Listening

The activities in this chapter aim to improve and practise the skills which students need in order to understand spoken English.

IMPROVING LISTENING SKILLS

When students listen to a cassette or to a person speaking, they can find it a challenge. This is because they have no visual clues and may think that they will not understand. Also, we usually only have one chance to hear something. This is why, as we saw in Chapter 5, before a listening exercise, we need to start by doing activities to prepare students. Then we need to do activities in which the students need to use the information from the item they have listened to. The main sub-skills of listening are:

1. predicting;
2. listening for the main idea(s);
3. listening for specific information.

To help improve listening, we plan a lesson in these phases:

1. Before-listening activities.
2. During-listening activities.
3. After-listening activities.

The purpose of these activities is to focus students' attention on the item they will listen to. You can tell them that they probably will not understand everything but that this does not matter.

'BEFORE-LISTENING' ACTIVITIES

A 'before-listening' activity needs to be short – five minutes at most. It can include any of the following ideas, but make sure you choose a different one in different lessons for variety and to keep students motivated.

Brainstorming

Discuss the title or topic of the item they will be listening to with the class. You or a student can write any important vocabulary on the blackboard, for future checking and reference.

Discussion

Ask the students to discuss among themselves a picture about the item they will be listening to, or the title. They can talk about what they think the topic will include, who could be in it, and what might happen. Encourage everyone to say something, by asking them to work in pairs or small groups.

Questioning

Students look at a picture related to the item they will listen to and think of questions that they would like answered. This gives useful practice in question formation, as well as giving students a reason to listen (to find out if their questions are answered).

Pre-teaching difficult key words

Sometimes you may want to teach students some of the difficult and important key words that they will hear (see Chapter 6 for ideas for teaching vocabulary).

'DURING-LISTENING' ACTIVITIES

To help students practise listening for *general information* only, ask them to listen and find out, for example:

- ▶ how many people are in the story or dialogue;
- ▶ who the story or dialogue is about;
- ▶ where the story or dialogue happened;
- ▶ when the story or dialogue happened.

Listening for *specific information* means students must learn to ignore the details. To practise this, you can ask the students to listen carefully for the answers to specific questions. They can more easily record the information required by filling in a chart copied from the blackboard. For example, students listen to people who have applied for a job and complete the chart in Figure 9.1 while they listen.

	Name	Age	Appearance	Character	Job
1					
2					
3					
4					

Figure 9.1

'AFTER-LISTENING' ACTIVITIES

In real life, we usually do something after we have listened to someone. So it is important to do some follow-up activities after listening, for example, students make up a similar dialogue, or discuss what they have heard in pairs or small groups. Students can write notes on what they thought they heard, and then compare their notes with a partner. Students could write a letter to a newspaper or radio station, giving opinions on what they heard.

Classroom Action Task Look at a listening exercise that you are going to do in class next week, and think of an appropriate 'before-listening' and 'after-listening' activity for your students.

10/ Ideas for Improving Reading

The activities in this chapter aim to improve and practise the skills that students need in order to read and understand English. At the end of this chapter we will also look at teaching literature.

IMPROVING READING SKILLS

Students reading in a second or foreign language usually try to read a text intensively, which means trying to understand every word. Intensive reading is something that many teachers know how to teach well. But as we saw in Chapter 5, this is not how we read in our first or main language. We often use other reading sub-skills, so we need to teach these sub-skills too. The main sub-skills of reading are:

1. predicting;
2. reading for the main idea(s);
3. reading for specific information.

To help improve reading, we plan a lesson in three parts:

1. Before-reading activities.
2. During-reading activities.
3. After-reading actvities.

'BEFORE-READING' ACTIVITIES

'Before-reading' activities should be short and focused – five minutes is usually long enough. They can include any of the following examples:

Brainstorming
Ask your students what words or ideas they can suggest that relate to the text that they will read, or to a picture from the text or to the topic or title. Either you or a student can write the words on the blackboard.

This will help them remember the words, and later they can look out for these words while reading.

Discussion

Ask your students to discuss a picture from the text or the title. They can talk about what they think the story will be about, who will be in it, and what might happen. To encourage everyone to take part in the discussion, get students to talk in pairs or small groups.

Questioning

Students look at a picture from the story, or at the title or first sentence from the text, and think of questions they would like answered about the story. This gives useful practice in question formation, and also gives them a reason to read, so that they can find out if their questions are answered.

Pre-teaching difficult key words

Sometimes you may feel it is a good idea to teach students some of the difficult and important key words from the story. You can quickly teach the words in the ways suggested in Chapter 6.

'DURING-READING' ACTIVITIES

Students need practice in the real-life activity of silent reading. If they are not used to reading silently, you can help them become better readers by giving a time limit. This encourages them to read more quickly and not to stop at unknown words.

It is best if the students do the actual reading individually or silently, as we do in real life. If you do not have enough books for each student to have their own, ask students to work in pairs or in small groups. Students take turns in being the 'silent reader' of their group and the others can ask questions about the text to find out what happens. If you only have one book, you can write some of the text on the blackboard. (Remember that if you read the text to the students, it then becomes a listening lesson!)

Here are some points to remember when doing reading with your class:

► Reading aloud is really pronunciation practice (see Chapter 13), and it can be time-consuming.
► Reading aloud is a natural way to read poems and plays.
► Reading aloud can be good for fluency practice and can build students' confidence if the text is not difficult for them.

Reading for the main idea

This means reading the whole text quickly to get the general idea of what it is about. To help students read quickly, give them a realistic time limit. Here are some activities.

Finding key words and topic sentences

For each paragraph or part of the story, students find the words or sentences that are the most important. This encourages them to not read the whole text in detail.

True or false sentences

The teacher or students write some true and some deliberately false sentences about the story on the blackboard. Then students check the text to find out which are correct.

Sequencing jumbled sentences or paragraphs

Write a few sentences about the text on the blackboard and ask the class to put them in the right order, as they read. Or write topic sentences and ask the class to match each one to a paragraph in the story.

Mid-text predicting

At points in the text when something dramatic or different has happened, or is going to happen soon, you can ask students to stop reading, close their book and to try to predict what might happen next. This encourages students to read carefully, imagine and discuss future possibilities, then read the next part to check their predictions.

Reading for specific information

Another way of reading a text is to look quickly at the whole text, but only read in detail the parts which give specific bits of information that you want. Here are some ideas.

Comprehension questions

Usually the teacher asks detailed questions about the text and the students say or write the answers. For variety, you can ask for written responses. This gives everyone an equal chance of answering. You can do this with the class working in small groups, with books closed to encourage discussion. In turn, the groups write their answers on the blackboard or tell the class. Students can make up their own questions in groups, then the questions are exchanged with another group. This activity also can be done by filling in a chart.

Gap-filling exercises

Remove all the verbs, or nouns, or adjectives, all the adverbs, or all the new or important words, from the text. Students have to guess the missing words from the context of the story. They can do this with or without a word bank (which lists the missing words but in random order).

Pronoun checks

Ask what the pronouns in the text refer back to. For example: he/she/it/they/we/his/hers/their/our. This recognition activity also shows the students how to use pronouns in their own writing.

Guessing unknown words

Students need to know how to deal with unknown words. This is very important because we will always find words we are not sure of, or do not recognise. Dealing with these kinds of words can help us enjoy reading, and become efficient readers. This is how to try and find out what to do with each unknown word:

► Decide if a word is important or not. Can you get the main idea without this word?
► Learn that you cannot always understand every word, and that it is not necessary to put equal importance on every word. Learn to ignore non-essential words.

If students decide that they really need to know the meaning of an unknown word, here are some techniques to try and work out the meaning:

► Guess an approximate meaning of the word from the context, which means looking at the words that can give clues. These can be found before or after the unknown word.
► Think about the possible meaning of the word from its roots, by removing the prefixes and suffixes, then see if it is word that you recognise.
► Does it look like a word in your first language? But be careful, as even if it does, it may mean something completely different!

'AFTER-READING' ACTIVITIES

As with listening, in real life we usually do something when we have read something. Here are some activities for students to do after reading.

- ▶ Retell the story in small groups or as a class. Students act out the story, using their own words.
- ▶ Rewrite the story in their own words, preferably in pairs or in groups to encourage discussion.
- ▶ Discuss the story in pairs or small groups, giving their opinions of what they have read, or suggesting different endings.

TEACHING LITERATURE

Teaching literature is about reading, but in a more extended way. Teaching literature in English is often a part of an English teacher's work, and students may need to pass exams about novels, plays or poems in English. Teaching literature begins as teaching reading skills and is often followed up with essay writing. So we can use the similar lesson phases of before-reading activities to prepare students for the reading, during-reading activities to explore the meaning of the text, and after-reading activities for students to relate to, or comment on what they have read and understood. Learning about literature usually includes writing about the text, in essay form, and often for national or international exams, so process writing techniques need to be taught and practised (see Chapter 11).

As learning about literature gives students cultural enrichment as well as language enrichment, we need to look at some ways that literature is taught. Some of the teaching approaches that are used to teach literature are:

- ▶ explaining or translating the text in great detail;
- ▶ giving the standard criticism of the text.

Students can be encouraged to read, understand and enjoy, and comment on the text more, and to learn to write good essays for exam questions. To begin with, it is not necessary or even possible to read the whole text in the class, especially if you only have one copy or a few copies of the text. Teaching literature needs to be a combination of classroom activities and out-of-class reading. The background to author and topic needs to be given. You can do this as a brief presentation, in notes or as a short research project by the students. You can give a brief outline of the main points of the story. This is particularly useful with Shakespeare texts, as there are usually sub-plots which can distract from the main ideas. You can give students edited highlights of the story or key scenes from a play. These, together with an early knowledge of the main characters, can help students to understand and develop a feeling for literature in English.

Students can read selected parts of the text in class, with a before-reading activity, during-reading activities and after-reading activities. They can have discussions in pairs and in groups, or act out in their own words important parts of the text and learn to write essays. The class and group discussions can be on the characters and their reactions to situations in the story, or interpreting the language. For example, identifying whether the language is literal or figurative: the literal 'She broke my arm' compared to the figurative 'She broke my heart'. Also, you and your students can discuss 'reading between the lines' or understanding the meaning of idiomatic language to find hidden thoughts and ideas.

Reading the text out-of-class can be done over an agreed period of time, when students take turns to read a part of the book. They need to learn to read quickly and then pass on the book, especially if theirs is the only copy of the book available. (For further ideas on sharing a book, see Chapter 20, on using limited resources.) Students can also make and fill in worksheets and then transfer that information to class display sheets, as they find out more about each character, each chapter and the story, such as:

▶ character information, including appearance, characteristics and relationship to other characters;
▶ who is in the chapter;
▶ what happened;
▶ when did this happen;
▶ why did this happen;
▶ what were the results;
▶ a storyline chart, on which the main action (and any sub-plots) of the play or story is noted as it happens.

Other material can help students with English literature; these are:

▶ a translation or a simplified version of the story to give students a general idea of the story-line;

▶ a video or film of the book or play;

▶ a similar story in your students' first or main language for comparison.

Learning to write essays for English literature exams can be done using the 'Process' writing skills (see Chapter 11).

The special work in teaching and learning to read English literature can involve the unusual but interesting use of language in the text. This can be the different language of older writers, such as Shakespeare, or the clever use of words in poems, with rhyming words, repetition and idiomatic language. Try to encourage your students to view the language of literature as something extra and special, to help them enjoy reading.

Classroom Action Task

Look at a reading text that you are going to do in class next week and plan two pre-reading activities.

Plan an easy and useful 'after-reading' activity for your students to do.

11 / Ideas for Improving Writing

You will remember that writing and speaking are called the 'productive' skills (see Chapter 3) and that we need to build up students' confidence by moving from controlled to guided activities. The activities in this chapter start with very teacher-controlled activities, and move to less teacher-controlled ones. (These activities correspond to the Practice and Production phases. The teacher does not need to do a long Presentation phase when focusing on writing skills.)

The activities will help students practise new language using writing, and also to start expressing their own ideas in writing. We also look at ways of teaching writing to more advanced students, who have to write essays for their exams, and how to correct written work.

PRACTICE PHASE

Controlled Practice
Copying correct sentences
Copying sentences helps students to practise new language and is also a good way to practise their writing skills. It is especially useful for students who normally write in a different script. Everything the students copy is correct and this is a motivating way to learn: it helps build confidence in their writing skills.

Students can copy correct sentences from the blackboard which illustrate new vocabulary, grammar or functional language. Then, to give students more involvement, you can ask them to suggest sentences. Help them to correct themselves and each other. You, or a student, write the final correct sentences on the blackboard for everyone to copy.

However, copying can become repetitive and students do not have to think, so it should not be used too often.

Matching beginnings and endings of sentences
Select a number of sentences (about five). You can use sentences from your coursebook, or make them up yourself. Write one half of each

sentence on the left of the blackboard, and the other half of the sentence on the right of the blackboard. Make sure that the two matching halves are not opposite each other. Label the sentences on the left with numbers (e.g. 1–5), and label the ones on the right with letters (e.g. A–E). The students then decide which two sentence halves go together to form a complete sentence, and they write down the number and the letter for each complete sentence. To quickly correct the work, you (or a student) can draw lines on the blackboard, joining the two correct parts of each sentence. It is then useful for students to copy out the correct sentences (Figure 11.1).

1. I went to the shop . . .	A. . . . to ask for a favour.
2. I washed my clothes . . .	B. . . . to get lots of sleep.
3. I went to bed early . . .	C. . . . to buy some bread.
4. I talked to my friend . . .	D. . . . to go to the party.

Figure 11.1

Substitution drills
This activity gives the students a basic correct sentence to learn from, but they have to make some choices in order to make complete and correct sentences.

Example: show students a picture of a cinema that is very full of people. Students should copy the following sentence, choosing and writing the correct word from the list.

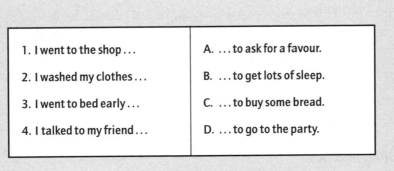

$$\begin{bmatrix} \text{The other day} \\ \text{Last night} \end{bmatrix} \text{Mum took us to the} \begin{bmatrix} \text{theatre} \\ \text{cinema} \end{bmatrix} \text{to see a} \begin{bmatrix} \text{film.} \\ \text{play.} \end{bmatrix}$$

$$\begin{bmatrix} \text{Luckily,} \\ \text{Unfortunately,} \end{bmatrix} \text{we} \begin{bmatrix} \text{were able to} \\ \text{couldn't} \end{bmatrix} \text{get good seats because the}$$

$$\begin{bmatrix} \text{theatre} \\ \text{cinema} \end{bmatrix} \text{was almost} \begin{bmatrix} \text{empty.} \\ \text{full.} \end{bmatrix}$$

Sequencing jumbled words

In this activity, jumbled words means that the correct words are provided, but in the wrong order. Write the words on the blackboard in random order. Students have to put the words in the right order. Ask the students to make sentences. The students then write them out in the correct order (Figure 11.2).

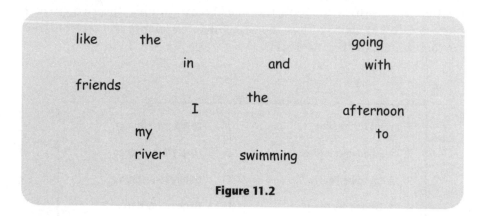

Figure 11.2

Guided practice

Gap-fill sentences

This is a more challenging activity, where students have to think of and write some of the words in sentences themselves. You can write the outline of the sentences on the blackboard, but with some words left out. The missing words can either be marked by a line or you can draw picture cues. The first time you do this activity, you could write the missing words in random order in a word-bank box at the side of the blackboard to guide the students. When your students become used to this activity, you can ask the class to just look at the gap-fill sentences on the blackboard, and try to remember the whole sentence, without writing anything down. Then you can rub out some more words, leaving a line for each missing word. The students then write out the full sentences from minimal word clues (Figure 11.3).

Changing sentences

This activity gives the basic correct sentences, but the students have to change a grammatical structure, for example from singular to plural, or to a different tense (Figure 11.4).

I _____ two sisters and _____

like going _____ school, because

we have _____ of friends and we like

_____ teacher.

we
our
lots
to
have

Figure 11.3

I like bananas, but I don't like oranges.

My friend _____ bananas, but she _____ oranges.

Figure 11.4

Completing sentences

You give the beginning of sentences and the students have to complete them. There may be several different correct suggestions and, as long as the grammar is correct, they are acceptable (Figure 11.5).

I am _____.

I like _____.

I have _____.

I live _____.

Figure 11.5

Parallel sentences

You write correct model sentences on the blackboard, and the students re-write the sentences, making it true for themselves, using the model sentences to get their grammar right (Figure 11.6).

My name is Alia and I am nine. I have three brothers and we live in a small house near the centre of the village

My name is . . .

Figure 11.6

Freer practice

Writing about pictures (one or a series)

The teacher uses a picture or a series of pictures to introduce the work and to help students think about the order of a situation or a story. A series of pictures helps with the staging of a story, or the teacher can ask questions to make sure the students understand the progress of the story. Go through the picture(s) with the students before they write anything, to check they understand the vocabulary. Write this vocabulary on the blackboard. The teacher can also ask for some ideas about what is happening in each picture. Students then write the story in their own words.

'Process-writing' approach

Process-writing is suitable for higher-level students preparing for exams. These students have to write longer compositions and essays with no time to work through a 'controlled to guided' series of writing activities. So, instead of moving step by step, students must learn to plan their writing. They learn that their first attempt is not the final product, but a beginning or first draft.

The teacher helps them with this process of writing by teaching them how to:

- find ideas or information for a composition;
- put these ideas or information in logical paragraphs;
- make sure the meaning is clear within these paragraphs;
- make sure the paragraphs are linked together well;
- make sure the language is accurate;
- make sure the language is appropriate to the purpose of the writing;
- find and correct errors in their work;
- improve each writing attempt (draft), so that the final draft is the best it can be.

Initially, the essay title can be brainstormed by the whole class, and a large range of facts and opinions are gathered and noted on the blackboard. Activities for getting ideas and information before writing include:

- listening to something about the topic, or a connected topic;
- reading a text connected to the writing topic;
- discussing the topic;
- showing a picture about the topic, and asking question about it;
- asking each other questions about the topic;
- writing down any vocabulary or ideas about the topic.

Planning the organisation of the essay

1. Outline the essay plan (introduction, outline topics, details of each topic, conclusion) with the whole class. The teacher or a student writes down the main points on the blackboard. Then the class discusses in pairs or groups how to logically order the points suggested.
2. Next, students write a first draft, either individually or as a group activity.
3. Make the first check on the writing. A correction code (see p. 76) saves a lot of time, and guides and encourages students to think about their mistakes. It is essential to teach a correction code for the process approach.

   Write your code on the blackboard, or on a large piece of paper near the blackboard. Give students an anonymous sample of work which you have corrected using your code, so they can practise correcting in a non-threatening way.

   You can use any code that you think is helpful. Here is an example:

T	=	wrong tense
G	=	wrong grammar
W	=	wrong word
^	=	missing word(s)
WO	=	wrong word order
S	=	wrong spelling
?	=	I don't understand

You start by underlining every mistake and use your code to note the type of mistake in the margin. The students then try to correct themselves. As students' writing improves and they get used to the code, you can leave out the code and only underline the mistakes (to show that there is a mistake), but students have to decide what type of mistake it is.

4. Students rewrite using the correction code and editing. Encourage students to work in pairs, asking each other for help and suggesting corrections. If they appear to be unhappy about working in this way, call it 'pair help' instead of 'pair correction'. You should persist in encouraging students to work in this way, as it is very important to try and set up a supportive learning atmosphere.

Classroom Action Task

Develop a suitable correction code and teach it to your students.

12/ Ideas for Improving Speaking

In this chapter we look at how teachers can help their students improve their speaking skills. We have seen that we can practise speaking either as part of a PPP lesson or as a separate lesson. In the Practice phase of the lesson, teachers help students to perfect their pronunciation by drilling and by correcting mistakes. You can plan to devote more time to the Practice phase if students continue to make a lot of mistakes. You can also plan a whole lesson to practise speaking. (See Chapter 13 for more detail about teaching and correcting pronunciation.)

PRESENTATION PHASE

As we saw in Chapter 5, in a lesson which practises speaking skills, students should only use language which they already know. It may be necessary for the teacher to check or pre-teach any vocabulary, grammar or functional language.

PRACTICE PHASE

Students work in pairs or small groups, as this gives all the class maximum opportunity for speaking practice. However, you should explain and monitor these activities carefully, so that the students get help when they need it.

Cued dialogue
You write an outline of a four- or six-line dialogue which you want students to say on the blackboard. Use cues, but do not write all the words (Figure 12.1).

Class questionnaires
You or the students make a list of words or pictures which suggest questions. Students work in groups, asking the question and making notes of the replies, and report on what their classmates said (Figure 12.2).

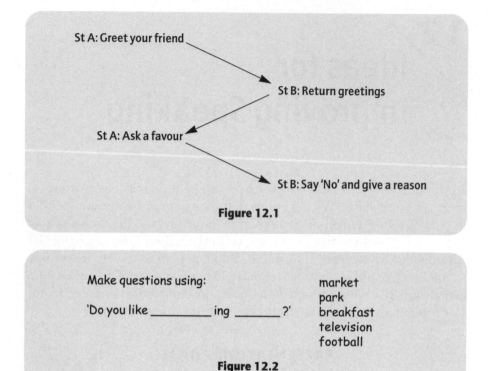

St A: Greet your friend

St B: Return greetings

St A: Ask a favour

St B: Say 'No' and give a reason

Figure 12.1

Make questions using:

'Do you like _____ ing _____ ?'

market
park
breakfast
television
football

Figure 12.2

Diary-filling

Ask each student to draw five diary pages in their notebooks. Students work on their own to fill in things they plan to do on five afternoons. Then talk with a partner and find out a time when they are both free to meet. Then they decide where they will meet (Figure 12.3).

Ordering activities

Make a list of favourite foods or activities on the blackboard. Individually, students put them in order of preference. Then, in pairs, students have to come to an agreement on their order of preference. Then, agree in groups of four to six students.

'Find the difference' pictures

Draw two simple pictures or diagrams on separate pieces of paper. Give the pieces to pairs of students or pin them up on different walls of the classroom. One student looks at one picture and the other at a different picture. Students ask each other questions to discover how the two pictures are different (Figure 12.4).

MY DIARY	Thursday
Monday	Friday Go shopping
Tuesday Visit Auntie	Saturday
Wednesday See doctor	Sunday

Figure 12.3

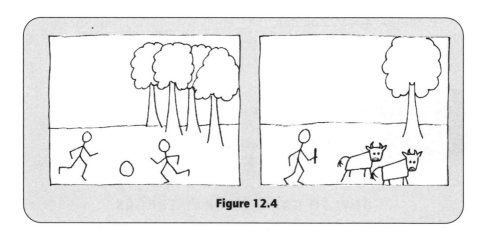

Figure 12.4

PRODUCTION PHASE

These activities lead on from the guided practice activities suggested above.

The cued dialogue can be used as a conversation starter: the students continue the dialogue in any way they want. Weaker students may require some guidance on what to talk about. At this stage, do not give them complete sentences, only possible topics.

The class questionnaires could be extended to talking about other likes and dislikes, or students can discuss their preferences.

The diary-filling exercise can be made freer by students talking about real-life activities that they are going to do in the near future, or students can discuss a real or possible joint activity in the future.

Ordering activities can be made more creative by asking students to discuss one of the topics in detail. Again, weaker students can be encouraged to talk with a few helpful questions about the chosen topic.

FEEDBACK FROM SPEAKING ACTIVITIES

There are two kinds of feedback that can result from a speaking activity:

1. *Feedback from other students*. Sometimes it is useful to ask the different groups to report on the discussions of their group, or to act out their dialogues, or to report on the results of their questionnaire.
2. *Feedback from the teacher*. While students are doing a speaking activity, it helps their confidence and fluency if you do not correct them. However, you can note any mistakes or communication problems, and then afterwards write them on the blackboard, so that the students can see what went wrong.

> **Classroom Action Task**
>
> Write a cued dialogue, using this situation:
> You meet a friend in the street, and you make an arrangement to meet at the weekend.

HOW TO CORRECT ORAL ERRORS

We have seen that during the Presentation phase, or during the early stages of the Practice phase of a lesson, the teacher corrects all errors. This is so that students know when they make mistakes in vocabulary, grammar or pronunciation. In the later stages of the Practice stage, teachers will continue to correct, but, as students improve, this will not happen so often. In the production or fluency stage, correction usually comes at the end of the lesson or at the beginning of the next lesson.

Students should not feel bad about making errors, so correction must be done positively and with encouragement. Students are learning when they make mistakes or help to correct other students' mistakes.

Correcting oral errors at the beginning of the lesson

▶ *When* must a teacher correct an error?
Directly after the student has made an error.

▶ *Who* should correct a student?
The teacher should point out the error and let the student try to correct himself first. Other students can also be asked to suggest a correct version

▶ *How* should teachers correct errors?
Here are some ideas you can try:

1. Let the student know there is an error.
   * Repeat the error and raise your eyebrow or make a facial expression to show that there is an error.
   * Ask other students: 'Do you like "I come yesterday" . . . ?'
   * Repeat the word with a rising intonation to suggest it is incorrect. 'I come . . . ?'
2. Help students to correct themselves and others.
   * Say 'Nearly'. Repeat and leave a gap for the student to correct him or herself.
   * Say 'Not . . . "I come yesterday" . . . but "I . . . . ?"'(wait for the student to correct him- or herself).
   * If the student does not know the correct form, the teacher can say 'Can anyone help?' and invite suggestions from other students.
   * Repeat the error and say: 'Tense?' or 'Stress?' or 'Pronunciation' (putting finger to mouth) to help the student correct herself or himself. (See Chapter 13 for guidance on correcting pronunciation.)
3. Finger correction
   * Use each finger of your left hand to represent a word. Holding your palm towards you, your little finger represents the first word of the sentence. Point to the 'words' with your right hand. Move from right to left so that the students 'read' from left to right.

Finger correction is often used for the following mistakes.

Missing words: for example, 'I've got car'. Point to the finger which represents the missing word 'a'.

Incorrect word: for example, 'I no like bananas'. Repeat the sentence, indicating a finger for each word. When you get to the incorrect one ('no') shake it with your right hand, repeating 'no' and say 'grammar', so that the student can correct herself or himself (Figure 12.5).

Missing contraction: for example, 'I have got a house'. Show the first three words with the fingers 'I have got . . .' and then squeeze the two fingers together to show the contraction 'I've . . .' (Figure 12.5).

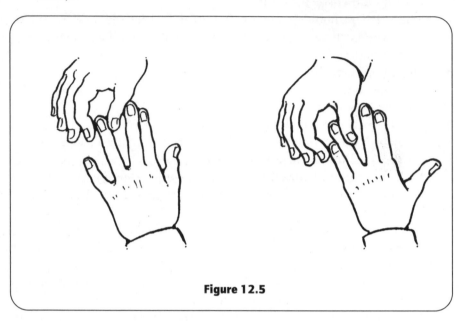

Figure 12.5

Correcting oral errors during less controlled and guided phases

Walk round discreetly, listening to the pairs or groups and quietly repeat the correct form when there is an error, giving the student time to repeat it and continue the flow of speech.

Correcting oral errors after the Production stage or fluency activity

During the activity, monitor the groups and discreetly make a written note of some errors you hear. At the end of the activity or the next day, put some of these on the board (do not say who made the mistake) and ask students to help you correct them.

Before or during activities, give out cards with 'Error spotter' written on it. The students who have these cards note down any errors they hear. You can also give cards with 'Well done' for students who spot particularly good phrases or vocabulary or persistent errors that are now corrected. This is one way of keeping your more advanced students involved in the activity. You can discuss the students' notes with the class at the end of the activity.

The PPP framework provides the opportunity for all learners to improve their accuracy and fluency. It is a good idea to tell your students when you expect them to be accurate and when you are giving them the chance to try out their fluency. This way they will understand why you sometimes correct them and sometimes you do not. In time, they will become used to the stages of the framework and understand your principles of correction.

Classroom Action Task

Make a note in your Teacher's Action Diary of one or two errors you hear in the classroom.

Now practise correcting these away from the classroom, preferably in front of a mirror using the finger correction techniques.

Try to use these techniques when you next go into a classroom.

13/ Ideas for Improving Pronunciation

In this chapter we look at how to improve the way students pronounce English so that other people can understand them more easily, and also at techniques for correcting pronunciation errors.

PRONUNCIATION

Let's start by looking at what we mean by pronunciation.

As we saw in Chapter 3, there are many acceptable varieties of English throughout the world. Whichever variety is used in your country, the most important thing is that students' pronunciation must be good enough for another person to understand what they are trying to say.

In a PPP lesson, teachers naturally include a good model of the pronunciation when they are presenting new vocabulary, grammar or functional language. It is important to start by helping your students recognise sounds before you expect them to produce them.

Spoken British English has 44 sounds, but there are only 26 letters in the alphabet for written English. This sometimes makes English pronunciation and spelling different, so it is not always best to write words on the blackboard at the early stages. Also, some sounds in English do not exist in some other languages. This can make it very difficult for students to recognise these sounds and even more difficult for them to pronounce them correctly. So some students need to do a lot of work on these sounds, listening to them, trying to recognise them and trying to copy them.

If you can understand and pronounce the symbols of the phonetic alphabet, this will help you to pronounce any word in the dictionary. You can teach this phonetic alphabet to your students and this will make teaching pronunciation much easier. However, you can teach pronunciation effectively without knowing the phonetic alphabet.

Pronouncing English well is not just about getting the individual sounds right. Students need to know:

- ▶ which parts of a word are stressed (spoken louder and longer);
- ▶ which parts of a sentence are stressed;
- ▶ basic intonation patterns;
- ▶ what it means when we change the intonation in a sentence (the music of the language);
- ▶ how to link together the sounds within a sentence.

Students need practice in all these areas to improve their pronunciation. Let's look at each in turn.

THE SOUNDS OF ENGLISH

Students can pick up the sounds of the language by listening to their teachers, from tapes, the radio or from the English they hear outside the classroom.

Helping students *hear* the sounds clearly

If students have problems, the teacher can help students to *hear* the sounds clearly by:

- ▶ saying the sound clearly on its own several times and asking students to repeat it;
- ▶ saying the sound in a word or sentence and asking students to repeat it;
- ▶ explaining in your first or main language how to produce the sound (what to do with the tongue and the teeth). You can use gestures, curving your hand to be the roof of your mouth and using the other hand flat as your tongue, or a drawing on the board, to help do this;
- ▶ contrasting the sound with a similar sound, so that students can clearly hear the difference.

Helping students *distinguish* between similar sounds

Some sounds may not exist in students' own languages. The teacher can help students *distinguish* between similar sounds by reading out pairs of words with only one difference between them. This exercise is called 'minimal pairs'.

Minimal pairs

The teacher reads out a mixture of words from a list which contain a common sound and the two contrasted sounds like 'law . . . raw/lay . . . ray/laze . . . rays/liver . . . river'. Students have to raise their right hand when they hear 'l' and their left hand when they hear 'r'.

This can also be done with the difficult sounds in the middle or at the end of the word like: 'climb . . . crime/file . . . fire/glass . . . grass . . .'.

Helping students *practise* similar or new sounds

The teacher writes a long list of contrasted words (minimal pairs) on the blackboard. Students work in pairs. Student A draws two columns in a notebook. The student writes 'l' at the top of one column and 'r' at the top of the other. Student B chooses a selection of words from the board at random and reads them out to Student A, who has to write them down in the correct column, e.g. 'l' or 'r'. Students can then check each other's lists.

WORD STRESS

All spoken words have sounds and syllables. For example, the word 'cat' has three sounds but only one syllable. The word 'cattle' has two syllables. The word 'catalogue' has three syllables, and 'caterpillar' has four syllables. In English, when a word has two or more syllables, one of these is stressed, that is, spoken more loudly and given a longer time. The other syllables are weak, that is, spoken softly and given little time.

If students have a good model, they will pick up most word stress patterns automatically. The rules for word stress are fairly complicated, but students should be aware of the importance of word stress because when a student uses an incorrect word stress pattern, the listener may not understand the meaning of what the student is trying to say.

Helping students *hear* word stress patterns

You can help students understand about word stress by using the sound 'da' for stressed syllables and 'di' for weak ones. So cat = da, cattle = da di, catalogue = da, di, di, and caterpillar = da di, di, di. You can also illustrate these stress patterns by loud and soft claps, or loud and soft taps on the desk.

You can help students practise hearing these patterns by writing a list of words of two or more syllables on the blackboard. Students copy these into their notebooks. Now read the words aloud. Students have to underline the stressed syllable in each word.

Word Stress Bingo

Write fifteen word patterns with different word stresses on the blackboard using 'O' for a stressed syllable and 'o' for an unstressed syllable, for example: Ooo (b<u>u</u>tterfly), ooOo (compet<u>i</u>tion). Students must make a chart with ten squares in their books and copy ten word patterns from the fifteen, putting one in each square. The teacher dictates a mixed selection of words from the board. When students hear one of the words on their card, they cross it off. The first student to cross out all words correctly is the winner.

Helping students to *practise* word stress patterns

To practise correct word stress, students can play Word Stress Bingo in groups, taking turns to give the dictation. Groups can discuss whether the dictation is correct.

SENTENCE STRESS

English has a very distinctive rhythm. This is because we also stress certain syllables within a sentence, not just within a word. To mark stress in a sentence, we make those syllables louder and longer, and also higher. This stress comes on the most important word or words in a sentence and these are usually nouns, verbs and sometimes adjectives and adverbs. Other little words, like 'on', 'a', 'for', and 'and' can almost disappear.

We can also change the meaning of what we say by stressing those syllables in a sentence that we want to make more important than the others. Maybe we want to emphasise something, or to express our surprise or to correct what someone else has said. For example:

'Thank you for the *wonderful* present' (stress on 'wonderful').
'Is it *true* that you were born in an *aeroplane*?' (stress on 'true' and 'aeroplane').
'No, I don't come from *Nairobi*, I come from *Harare*' (stress on 'Nairobi' and 'Harare').

This example shows how you can change the meaning of the same sentences by changing the sentence stress.

'I saw Ayesha teaching in the *library*' (not the classroom).
'I saw *Ayesha* teaching in the library' (usually I see Leila teaching in the library).
'I saw Ayesha *teaching* in the library' (she usually tidies up the books).

LINKING SOUNDS IN ENGLISH

In English, the length of time between all stressed syllables is about the same, so all the rest of the sentence (the words that are weak or unstressed) gets even weaker and has to be slurred together so that the beat keeps regular. Look at the chart in Figure 13.1.

Number of syllables		Number of beats
2	<u>Come</u> home	2
5	You <u>ought</u> to come <u>home</u>	2
7	You <u>ought</u> to have been at <u>home</u>	2

Figure 13.1

Do you see how all those syllables in the last examples have to be squeezed into two beats?

You can demonstrate this to students by speaking and showing the beat with your hand. A poem or a chant with a good rhythm can demonstrate this. Rhymes that students use for skipping with a rope are especially good. The way for students to practise stressing some syllables in sentences and making other groups of words weak is by drilling and learning rhymes like this one (Figure 13.2).

one	two	buckle my	shoe
three	four	knock at the	door
five	six	pick up	sticks
seven	eight	lay them	straight
nine	ten	a big fat	hen

Figure 13.2

INTONATION

Intonation is the formal word for the music of English; that is, how our voice rises and falls at certain different parts of sentences. There are certain rules, such as those for asking questions and finishing sentences, but, as with sentence stress, we can express emotions like surprise, sympathy, anger, delight, etc., by changing our intonation pattern. For example, a rising tone is used:

▶ When asking questions that are answered 'Yes' or 'No': 'Is he your cousin?'. 'Would you like some tea?', 'Are you comfortable?'.
▶ To express surprise, interest or disbelief: 'Really?', 'Did you?', 'What?'.

A falling tone is used:

▶ For ending normal statements: 'I really like cassava'. 'It's so hot again today'.
▶ For questions which begin with What, When, Where, Who, Which, Why and How: 'What's your name?', 'When are you going?', 'How do you come to school?'.

Students will learn these and other intonation patterns by listening to a good model and repeating. As you present some new language, you can show the rise and fall of the intonation pattern by arm and hand movements. When you write a sentence on the board you can show the intonation by writing in the arrows as in the above examples.

Helping students *practise* intonation and sentence stress patterns

You can help students practise intonation and sentence stress patterns by organising chain drills round the class or groups. Students can practise asking and answering questions. It is fun to tell students some surprising information and ask them to respond with the correct phrase and intonation. Then they themselves can make up 'crazy statements' for others in their group who have to respond with the correct intonation, for example:

Teacher: 'My grandmother is 117'.   Student: 'Really?'.
Teacher: 'I went to the cinema six times last week'.   Student: 'Did you?'.

When teaching pronunciation remember:

▶ Give students the chance to recognise sounds and patterns before you ask them to reproduce them.

▶ Students must know about the stressed and unstressed parts of a sentence so that they can get the rhythm of English right.

▶ Sentence stress tells us which parts of the statement are important.

▶ We can change the meaning of a sentence by changing the stress and intonation.

▶ Correct word and sentence stress and intonation are just as important as getting the individual sounds right.

Classroom Action Task

Can you think of any sounds in English that do not appear in your language?

Can you think of any sounds in your language that do not appear in English?

Prepare a Bingo game using word stress patterns you have taught.

Ask your students to tell you a skipping rhyme in your language. See if they can write one in English.

14 / Role Plays, Projects and Presentations

All students of English, whether they are intermediate, advanced or beginners, need to have a lot of practice using their English freely in the classroom to practise the language they have learned.

Activities like group discussion and answering questions in class give students a chance to practise speaking English fluently. But sometimes, only confident students take part. Many more students will be able to practise communicating when they work simultaneously in pairs or in groups of up to four during the lessons. These activities, which include role plays, projects and presentations, should be planned for the Production phase of a lesson. For advanced students, these activities can be planned to fill a whole lesson or series of lessons.

The objective of these types of production activities is to improve the students' fluency in English without the immediate help of the teacher, so it is very important that the students are well prepared. You must be sure that the following points are covered:

▶ The first time students do a simulation or a role play, the language content must be very easy.
▶ Students must know enough vocabulary to do the activity.
▶ Students must have learned enough correct grammar or appropriate functional language to be able to do the activity.
▶ Students must have enough knowledge of the topic to be able to do the activity.
▶ Students must be able to finish the task successfully.
▶ Instructions for the activity must be very clear. The teacher can give these very clearly in the students' first or main language. Instructions can also be written on the blackboard. Teachers must check that students understand what they have to do.
▶ Activities must not be too long.
▶ Teachers must organise the activity so that students at all levels of ability have a part to play and benefit from the activity.
▶ The teacher does not correct during the activity, but can watch and note errors during the activity and correct when it is finished.

SIMULATIONS, ROLE PLAYS AND DRAMA

These three activities are very similar. For all three, students should be given time to prepare by reviewing the language and the information that they need in order to do the activity. For intermediate students, you can prepare these notes together as a class. Advanced students can make notes alone, in pairs or in groups, before they start the activity.

Simulations

In a simulation, students express their reactions to a fictitious (imaginary) situation using their own words and opinions.

Example (students work in groups of four)
Someone has donated a large sum of money to your school or college. Imagine that you are all members of the committee. One person is the chairperson. Decide how this money should be spent. When the meeting is over, each group can tell another group its plan, or can write up the minutes of the meeting.

The type of language that students need to be taught in the lessons before this activity includes the language of holding a meeting, how to express opinions, agreeing and disagreeing, planning.

Role plays

In a role play, students are given a part to play in a fictitious situation. They have to act out the role of their character. Role plays are useful because students have to think about how their character will react. Also, some students participate better when they are pretending to be someone else. A few props may motivate students to play their characters.

Class preparation is necessary to check that students know the language and the information that is needed to do the activity. The teacher can decide on the roles before the class and give out role cards with information about the situation or problem, and even how characters should behave (Figure 14.1).

If it is not possible to hand out cards, then useful vocabulary and phrases and other information can be written on the blackboard.

Example of role play activity (students work in pairs or groups)
One of you is a famous person. The other(s) is/are a reporter(s) from the local newspaper. The reporter(s) must think up questions for the famous person and then interview him. Each group could interview a famous person of their choice, or all the class could interview the same

STUDENT A: You grew up in a city. You want to build a factory that needs water. You want to buy land from student B. You will employ a lot of people and pay quite well, but the work is dull.	STUDENT B: Your farm is near the river. All your family works on the farm and recently it has been very successful. You sell a lot of vegetables at the local market. No one in your family wants to work in the factory. Your son wants money to go to college.

Figure 14.1

famous person. Afterwards the famous person can help the reporter write the article for his newspaper.

Examples of language learned during the lesson/unit of teaching before the role play:

► asking questions;
► asking about likes and dislikes;
► asking about past, present and future plans;
► telling about likes and dislikes.

Put a large sheet of paper at the back or side of the classroom (if this is impossible, divide the blackboard, with half the information on one side and the other half of the information on the other side). You can write the different bits of information on the sheets of paper, or on the different halves of the blackboard. Ask half the students to look at one part of the information and the rest of the students to look at the rest of the information. This type of information gap activity means that the students have to talk to each other, each using their different information.

Drama

A drama activity is in many ways a grander version of a role play. Drama for language practice does not always mean learning a script by heart and performing it. Students can improvise and create a drama for themselves, using language they have already learned. They need to do some preparation and may need to practise improvisation. They can do this preparation in groups and perform their improvisation to other groups, to the rest of the class or even to the rest of the school. The presentation of a play is especially good if the school celebrates an English Day or if an English Club wants to promote its activities.

You can get ideas for drama performances from a situation or a text in the students' coursebook or from some literature they are studying. It can be motivating for students to act out an incident which appears in a local newspaper or magazine. Students can take the part of the main characters in the situation. A small selection of objects or some pictures can form the basis of a story which students invent and then act out. Four chairs, arranged in different ways (a waiting room, a car, a cinema, a table in a restaurant) can prompt some ideas for students to act out a disagreement, an amusing story or a minor disaster.

PROJECT WORK

Project work complements other, more formal methods of learning. When doing project work, students have to produce an extended piece of work with only limited guidance from the teacher. The students have to find out the information they need from the resources that the teacher supplies. The teacher may also tell students where they can find information for the task. The students then have to put the relevant information together to produce an end-product.

This approach can be adapted to almost all levels, ages and abilities and is therefore very suited to large classes with students of mixed abilities. Although the teacher often has to do a lot of preparatory work, the students should be able to work alone at a pace which suits them and following their individual interests. Of course, all students have to finish the project at the stated time. Project work is a good way of helping students develop good study skills and to integrate their reading, writing, speaking and listening. Projects can be done as homework, as a special assignment or in the classroom. Project work often links the classroom with the real world, so it is a good preparation for using English outside school.

First the teacher and the students have to decide what this end-product should be. The choice depends on the level and interests of the students and the resources available. Here is a list of some end-products that students have done:

▶ An individual file with texts, some written by students themselves, and pictures either drawn by students or cut out of magazines about their favourite animals.
▶ A class newspaper or magazine with articles, drawings and possibly photos taken by students.

▶ A class profile.
▶ A tourist guide to the town where students live.
▶ Organising some activities for an English Day.
▶ An exhibition with pictures, posters and text about how young people spend their leisure time.
▶ A series of presentations about the customs of an English-speaking country.
▶ A radio programme about the institutions in an English-speaking country.

Planning a project

A project must be carefully planned. The teacher must think about all the following points:

▶ What will the topic be?
▶ What will the end-product be? For example, a newsletter, a radio programme, a portfolio, a newspaper, an exhibition, some presentations, or some activities for an English Day?
▶ What about the organisation? How long should the project last? A shorter project that is easily completed is more motivating than one that lasts many weeks.
▶ How should the participants be grouped? Alone, in pairs, in small groups, in mixed-ability groups?
▶ How many stages should the project have? What will happen at each stage and where will they take place?
▶ What resources are available? What books, magazines, pictures, etc., are available and what people could be interviewed?
▶ How much work should be done in the classroom, the school, or the library? Can the participants get information from their families or from the community?
▶ What constraints are there? Do students need money to carry out their investigations? Is it an appropriate time of year to do a project? Do students have other commitments and is the weather suitable? Can you get paper, files or pictures? Do you need a tape recorder? Do you have one?
▶ Are you going to assess the project? Will there be a single mark at the end or will students get marks as their project progresses? What grading system will you use? Will students who work together in a group get the same mark? Will you give a mark for effort, or for participation, or only for the end-product?

Look at this example of a teacher's plan for a project on 'A young person's guide to our town'.

1. *End-product*: a booklet which can be reproduced cheaply.
2. *Contents*: places to eat and drink, tourist attractions, where to get help and advice, getting around (transport), where to meet other young people, 'value-for-money' shops, discos, clubs, cinemas; history/famous inhabitants, sports facilities, maps and shortcuts around the town.
3. *Summary of stages* (Figure 14.2).

1. Class discussion	Idea of project	½–1 hour
2. Group discussions	Group plans	½–1 hour
3. Research/Writing	Information in note form	1½–2 hours
4. Writing/Proofreading	First draft of guide	1½–2 hours
5. Discussion/Rewriting	Final texts/Agreed format	1–1½ hours
6. Reporting/Discussion	Display	1 hour
7. Production	The Town Guide	2–3 hours
	Total anticipated time	8–11½ hours

Figure 14.2

4. *Resources*: existing town guides, maps, local newspapers, access to a typewriter and copying facilities, local library, tourist information offices, older inhabitants of the town.
5. *Location*:
   - Stages 1, 2, 3, 6, 7 – the classroom.
   - Stage 3 – town (in or out of school time).
   - Stages 4, 5 – classroom or home.

(Adapted from *Projects for the EFL Classroom* by Simon Haines.)

PRESENTATIONS

It is very useful for students to learn to give short presentations to the rest of the class. This kind of skill may be very important if students go on to study at college or university or have to do a job interview in English. A simple presentation can be an activity like bringing in a favourite object and telling the rest of the class or group some information about it for two or three minutes. This information could be: why you have chosen it, what memories it brings back, what it is made of, how it works, what it is normally used for, other possible uses, some facts about its history and so on. In a more complicated presentation, a student can use visual aids, like a poster, the blackboard or an overhead projector.

Even if a presentation is very simple, the teacher gives the speaker feedback (tell the speaker what is good and what needs to be better about the presentation).

The teacher can comment on presentation skills such as:

► Does the speaker stand or sit where all the listeners can see her?
► Are any visual aids or objects clearly understandable and easily seen?
► Do the visual aids help comprehension?
► Is the information well-sequenced?
► Is the speaker easy to hear?
► Does the speaker keep eye contact with the listeners?
► Does the speaker check that her listeners understand?
► Does the speaker leave time for questions?
► Does the speaker fit all of the presentation into the time allowed?
► Is the speaker's use of English correct and appropriate?

A presentation is a very good end-product for a project. But it can also be used for other fluency activities such as the end of a role play or simulation, when one person presents the results of a discussion to the rest of the class or group; for example, how the money is to be spent (see page 92). At a more advanced level, students can report back on work they have been set to do or on some literature they have read. When students are familiar with doing presentations, the teacher can invite the rest of the class to join in the feedback and this will reinforce their knowledge of what makes a good presentation.

Now that you know about the need for fluency practice in the classroom, be sure to build some activities of this kind into the Production phase of your lesson plan. If your students are not used to communicating with each other in the classroom, you may need to start with very short, enjoyable fluency activities.

Classroom Action Task	Decide on a short activity and try it out in class.
	In your Teacher's Action Diary, make a note of when and how you introduced fluency activities. What was the reaction of your students after the first time? And after the second and third time? Discuss their progress with other colleagues.

15/Testing

Many tests and exams are written by the Ministry or other educational institutions. But you may need to set tests to check that your students have learned what you have taught them or to find out if your teaching is effective. You may also set tests as practice for external exams. In this case, you must be sure that the type of questions you set are compatible with those in the external exam.

In this chapter we look at areas of language learning we can test. We shall think about how to write or organise a good reliable test and look at some examples of different kinds of questions and activities you can use if you have to organise tests for your students.

TESTING LANGUAGE

You may want to test your students' knowledge of vocabulary, grammar and functional language. You may also need to test them on their use of this knowledge, as well as their competence in the skills of listening, speaking, reading and writing in English. You can also test their pronunciation.

A good test

Sometimes test results are disappointing. This is not always because the students have not studied well. Maybe the test is just too difficult. Maybe the teaching needs to be improved! Remember: success motivates students. You need to know how to make a good test.

When you write a test make sure that you carry out the instructions in Figure 15.1.

PREPARING TESTS AND EXAMS

Many tests focus on grammar and vocabulary, but it is important to test the use of functional language, pronunciation and the four language skills as well. You can use many of the activities and exercises that your

Only test the language and skills the students have already learnt.	So check the syllabus or the learning objectives of the lesson to make sure you have covered the work you intend to test.
Write very simple, clear instructions.	All students must be able to understand them and must have done the type of question or task before. For example, have they used multiple-choice or gap-fill before? Give an example with an answer on the test paper.
Decide on a marking scheme that is objective.	Make sure that if whoever were to mark the test, students would still get the same marks.
Decide on a reasonable pass mark.	It is no good students doing a test which is so difficult that most of them fail. This happens sometimes with national exams. Remember, success motivates your students.
Write on the test paper exactly how many marks students will get for each question.	For example, will they get marks for correct grammar, correct spelling, good content, tidy writing, or all of these things?
A test should be very easy for the teacher to mark.	You may have to mark hundreds of papers, so have a look at Chapter 17 to learn more about how to do this easily.

Figure 15.1

students do in the Practice phase of a lesson or the 'during' phase of a reading or listening lesson to test your students; but remember, this time the purpose is to test, not teach.

Here are some examples of question types and tasks.

Testing grammar
See Figure 15.2.

Testing vocabulary
See Figure 15.3.

Question form	Example
Give the correct form	Write these verbs in the present perfect: he speaks, he lives, he gives, etc.
Write a complete sentence	I / go / city / visit / brother / Thursday
Fill in the gaps using the verbs below in the past tense	Bosede ... for Nigerian Airways She ... French and English She ... four times a week works / flies / speaks

Figure 15.2

Choose the correct word	Mary looks ... her baby sister every evening a) for b) after c) at d) over
Look at the pictures and circle True (T) or False (F)	SILVIJA MARINA Silvija is wearing glasses T F Marina has straight hair T F Marina is wearing a necklace T F Silvija has curly hair T F
Put the words in the correct column	stride whisper stumble stagger call yell trip march shout Speaking | Walking

Figure 15.3

Testing functional language

You are lost and you ask someone the way. What do you say? Circle a, b or c:

a) 'Where must I go to the station?'
b) 'Excuse me, where is the station?'
c) 'Tell me where the station is, please.'

It is your friend's birthday. Tick the correct thing to say to him:

a) 'Congratulations.'
b) 'Happy birthday.'
c) 'Have a nice day.'

Draw a line to show the best way of speaking to the people in Column B:

A	B
'Have you got a pen?'	A stranger
'Could I borrow your pen, please?'	Your teacher
'I'm sorry to trouble you, but could I borrow a pen?'	Your friend

Testing pronunciation

Underline the stressed syllables in these words:

a) photograph
b) artist
c) incorrect

Matching sounds

Put a circle round the words with the same sounds in the middle of the word:

a) bear
b) fair
c) foot
d) read
e) where
f) lead

Sentence stress

Underline the main stress in these sentences:

a) My uncle is a doctor, not a dentist.
b) He is a friendly dog. He won't bite you.
c) If your friend is away from home, you can come and stay at my home.

Testing language skills

You can use any of the activities and exercises that you normally use to practise reading, writing, listening and speaking. But make a note of the following points.

Testing reading

▶ Choose texts that are based on students' own life or knowledge.
▶ Do not use texts that students have already seen. These test their memory, not their reading skills.

Testing listening

▶ Dictation is a useful form of listening test. Make sure everyone can hear you or the tape recorder. Do a trial run to check this.
▶ Set the context of the listening as you would in listening practice.
▶ Write and read your own listening tasks so you are sure you are testing what students have learnt.
▶ Don't forget: you can include a test of test students' recognition of similar sounds (see Chapter 13).

Testing writing

The way you test this will depend on the writing approach you have been using with your students (see Chapter 11). If you have used controlled and guided activities, you may write some tests that are very similar to those suggested in the chapters on teaching writing and grammar. If you use a process-writing approach, the way you give marks may be different. Decide what marks you give for accurate writing, correct content, creativity or appropriate style and tell the students this on the exam paper. Always state the number of words required.

Testing speaking

► When you construct the test, be clear what you are giving marks for. You can give marks for grammatical accuracy, using vocabulary you have taught them, using appropriate functional language, pronunciation, etc.

► Make a record sheet like the one below so that you can record all the things you want to test and how well a student performs it (1 point, 2 points, 3 or 4).

	1	2	3	4
Pronunciation				
Functions				
Vocabulary				
Grammar				

Figure 15.4

Organising speaking tests

If you have a large class, you need to plan very carefully the way you test speaking. Here are some ideas to help you:

► Do the testing over many lessons.

► Test students in groups of two or three. Be careful how you group students in case stronger students always dominate weaker ones in the group.

► Decide if you are going to give a group mark or an individual mark.

► Give all students a writing activity or test and call out individuals or groups to test them where they cannot disturb the writers.

► Always mark speaking as it happens or very soon afterwards. You will quickly forget what level a student actually achieved.

► Use cards marked with topics for discussion, pictures, maps, diagrams or objects to give students something to talk about. These will also make them feel more relaxed.

► If you record speaking tests, don't forget to ask students to say their names.

Classroom Action Task

Have a look at past tests that students have done.

Compare them with a syllabus or course book if you have one.

Do they have the qualities of a good test?

How would you change them to make them better?

Discuss this with other teachers.

16 Planning and Classroom Organisation

In this chapter we will suggest some general classroom management techniques which will help you in your present teaching situation and which will also help you to overcome new challenges as you involve your students more in the learning process.

The following chapter contains practical examples and activities to help you put these techniques into practice in your classroom.

CLASSROOM MANAGEMENT IN LARGE CLASSES

In a large class, good classroom management techniques are particularly important. Good classroom management makes your job easier and helps students to learn better. We also want to train our students to co-operate in our classroom management.

Often it is teachers who do not like large classes. As we saw in Chapter 1, the main challenges for teachers of managing learning in large classes are:

▶ dealing with a wide range of ages and abilities;
▶ keeping everyone's attention;
▶ doing oral work;
▶ students' motivation to learn English may be poor;
▶ helping weaker students;
▶ checking individual progress;
▶ attendance and continuity;
▶ marking large quantities of written work;
▶ taking the register.

Some students like being part of a large class because it is 'safe': there are lots of students to do the work and the teacher cannot watch and listen to everyone. However, other students in a large class want more contact and help from the teacher.

There is no 'big answer' to solve the challenges, but there are lots of 'small answers'. Teachers all over the world have contributed many tried and tested tips to help you and your students get used to new teaching methodologies which can improve their learning.

Classroom management involves:

▶ planning lessons which include variety and which meet objectives;
▶ giving clear instructions to students on what you want them to do;
▶ setting up and monitoring student interactions in pair and group work;
▶ using teaching and learning resources;
▶ moving clearly from one phase of the lesson to the next phase;
▶ timing and balancing of learning activities;
▶ starting and finishing the lesson.

PLANNING

Good classroom management starts with planning. Planning is one of the most important and most helpful things that teachers can do. Effective planning means that teachers, students, parents and principals know what will be learnt, when it will be learnt, and how learning will take place.

Start by thinking of the work you have to do in each year, each term, each week and each lesson. Your Ministry of Education or your course book may have a syllabus: this is the amount of work you have to teach in a year. The division of all this work is called a 'scheme of work' – these are sometimes provided by the Ministry, or you may make your own. It is not difficult, but you need to sit down before the year (or term) starts, with a piece of paper that will clearly show all you will be teaching. It is helpful to use a pencil as you will need to keep rubbing out, moving and changing things in order to make them fit.

You need to think about:

▶ how much work you have to finish with each class by the end of the academic year;
▶ how you will divide this work into what you will have to finish each term;
▶ how you will divide each term's work into what you will have to finish each week;
▶ how you will divide each week's work into what you will have to finish each lesson.

When you have done this outline, you will have thought about the work that you have to do both in the long and the short term. If you plan teaching in good time, you will always know if you are getting behind or ahead with the work you have to do. If some parts of the work you have to finish take longer than you originally planned, then all you have to do is readjust the rest of the week's work (see Figure 16.1).

WEEKS	TERM 1: Scheme of work	
Week 1	Unit 1	• If you have to complete four units in a term, here is a way of dividing up the work.
Week 2		• Do not spend more time than noted on each unit.
	Catch-up day	• Between each unit, plan a 'catch-up' day to fill in for classes missed or to give students extra lessons for a challenging unit.
Week 3	Unit 2	
Week 4		
Week 5	Revision	• Plan a revision lesson before the tests.
	Half-term test	• Remember – plan carefully, but be flexible!
Week 6	Unit 3	
Week 7		
	Catch-up day	
Week 8		
	Unit 4	
Week 9		
Week 10	Revision	
	End-of-term test	

Figure 16.1

The scheme of work should also show days and dates, classes and subjects, and the approximate work for each week in each subject. Remember: the main purpose of a scheme of work is to help you keep control of *what* needs to be taught and *when* it needs to be taught.

All planning needs to allow for things that will change. Some events are out of our control; for example, the school may have to close for a week because of heavy rains. Maybe the whole class finds the work easy and finishes early. Or you may have to spend longer than you planned on one part of the lesson, because the class finds it difficult. To allow for unexpected spare time or for shortage of time in any lesson, always have an extra activity ready and identify one activity that you can leave out of a lesson.

Sometimes it is difficult to finish the syllabus in the time given; but the syllabus and the length of the school year cannot be changed. So think positively and plan ahead to make sure that there is enough time to finish all the work, without a panic at the end. Planning is always time very well spent.

LESSON PLANS

After you have planned your scheme of work for each class, you will then need to think about each individual lesson and make a lesson plan. With a little practice, this will not take long. Lesson plans make teaching and learning easier for both teacher and students.

We need to learn to make and use lesson plans, because they:

▶ make teaching easier;
▶ help us get through our lesson, without forgetting important phases;
▶ are a permanent written record of what we have taught;
▶ remind us which class we taught and when we taught that lesson;
▶ include class size, and resources we used.

Here are the areas you need to think about when planning a lesson:

▶ What is the objective of the lesson – what will the students learn?
▶ Will the objective of the lesson be: learning vocabulary, grammar, functional language, or improving listening, speaking, reading or writing?
▶ What variety of activities will you use?
▶ How much time will each part of the lesson take?
▶ How will you manage the lesson – what you say, how you will group the students?
▶ If your students find the lesson too easy or too difficult, what will you do?
▶ How will you know if you have achieved the objective of your lesson?

Refer back to the lesson frameworks we looked at in Chapters 4 and 5 and look at the example of a lesson plan in Figure 16.2. The most important parts to look at are the headings and the timing breakdown of the lesson.

LESSON PLAN	DATE:
No. in class:	38
Language objective:	Making requests and replying with an offer of help
Resources used:	pencils/books/a box
Time:	30 minutes

Lesson phase	Student and teacher interaction	Time
<u>Presentation</u> Teach 'Could you ... lend me a pencil/a book/ open the door.' 'Yes of course.'	T ⟶ Sts Sts ⟶ T	10 min
<u>Practice</u> Drill requests as a class, then rows, then pairs	T ⟶ Sts Sts ⟶ T Sts ⟶ Sts	10 min
<u>Production</u> Students think of own requests and ask each other Homework	Sts ⟶ Sts	10 min

Figure 16.2

We know that in each lesson, we need to plan time to:

▶ ask about and review previous learning;
▶ present new language;
▶ practise new language;
▶ produce new language;
▶ improve language skills.

We also need to plan each lesson to include a balance between:

- ▶ teacher talking-time and student participation;
- ▶ learning and practising both new language and previously learned language (previously learned language needs continual practice);
- ▶ listening, speaking, reading and writing activities;
- ▶ knowing about language and learning how to use language.

It is very important to have variety and balance for effective learning. If any of these areas of teaching and learning become unbalanced over a period of several lessons, students may become bored and they may stop learning.

Planning for variety

Each lesson should include a good variety of learning activities. This will help keep students interested and improve their motivation. Variety is also important in a large class because it gives all students a chance to benefit. As we saw in Chapter 1, each student has a different way of learning. So if we use only one type of activity, then only the students who enjoy or excel at this type of activity will benefit. If we use a wide variety of activities, then all students can find something they are good at or enjoy doing. This gives all students an opportunity to learn better.

We can plan for variety by thinking about:

- ▶ a variety of Presentation, Practice and Production techniques and activities;
- ▶ how much student participation we include;
- ▶ how much listening, speaking, reading or writing activities students do;
- ▶ how much pair or in-group work there is;
- ▶ how much language is cued in words, gesture or pictures;
- ▶ how much feedback from activities there is, to the teacher or to other students;
- ▶ how much correction there is, when the correction is done, and who does the correction.

Planning a variety of activities helps to keep students interested and motivated to learn better. Some tips you can use to increase the motivation of your students include:

- ▶ using students' own opinions, ideas and experiences;
- ▶ encouraging student contribution and letting them speak or write without fear;

- ► giving positive praise;
- ► planning learning in easily achievable steps;
- ► recognising and openly acknowledging individual and class progress;
- ► making best use of learning opportunities, both in and out of the classroom;
- ► emphasising the importance of English in your country, and for global communication;
- ► giving attention to all the students, not favouring the best, or the loudest;
- ► encouraging all students and giving lots of praise, especially to students who are working hard and trying to improve, and students lacking confidence. Do not use negative words or a discouraging tone of voice;
- ► carefully managing learning activities so that all students are involved, not just the quick and confident ones;
- ► making sure that any pair or group work benefits most of your class.

Classroom Action Task	Start planning by making a chart for the work you have to do next week, then:

Classroom Action Task

Start planning by making a chart for the work you have to do next week, then:

- • look at your text book and decide what you will teach every day;
- • think about each lesson and what you will teach;
- • use this plan every day before each lesson, to check what you must teach;
- • check this plan after each lesson to see if you have done what you planned;
- • if something was missed out, make sure you include it in the following week.

CLASSROOM MANAGEMENT

In all language lessons, the teacher is in control in different ways throughout the lesson. However, there are specific classroom management skills which help the lesson go well, particularly if your class is large.

Being clearly seen and heard

When you need to present new language or give instructions, make sure that you have the complete attention of all the students all the time. You may think you have all students' attention if you stand at the front of the class, but this is not always true. Students at the sides and back of the class may think that you cannot see what they are doing. If you always stand or sit in the same place, students may either feel neglected by the teacher, or think that they cannot be seen and may misbehave.

Make sure that all students can see you, and that you can be seen. This way, the class knows that you want to see everyone and that you are available when any student needs help, not just those sitting in the front row. Move around in your classroom as much as you can, slowly and quietly, so students are not disturbed and do not feel threatened.

It is very important to make sure that all students can hear you. If students at the back of the class cannot hear you very well, they may feel you do not care about them and so may stop learning. Project your voice so that students at the back of your class can hear you. Projecting your voice means speaking clearly and loudly, but not shouting. Practise with a colleague who sits at the back of your classroom. Your voice will be clearer and louder if you look up as you speak. Eye contact helps to make people understand that you are talking to them, but move your eyes around the class from time to time, and do not develop favourite students. Do not talk to the blackboard as you are writing on it. Learn to write while standing sideways-on to the blackboard.

Learning and using students' names

One of the best ways to gain and keep control and maintain discipline is to learn and use the students' names. Although it can be a challenge to quickly learn all the names of your students, especially if you have a large class, here is a technique to help you. Ask students to help you make a class plan on a piece of paper with all the names written on it, that you can hold and constantly refer to. To make this idea work, everyone sits in the same place until you tell them to change places.

Setting up your own classroom rules

Classroom rules help to establish and maintain good discipline. These classroom rules are in addition to school rules. You can discuss and agree class rules for behaviour that is acceptable in your classroom. These rules can then be put on the wall as a reminder for everyone. Take time to make sure that everyone understands and knows that they have to keep them. Students who do not keep these rules will be punished. It is a good idea to have different levels of discipline, starting with a warning and then using appropriate punishment. Often, removing a student's privileges can act as a good punishment. If you wish, good behaviour can be rewarded, especially good behaviour from students who are consistent offenders (Figure 16.3).

CLASS RULES

Enter and leave the class quietly.
Lessons start on time.
Speak English as much as possible.
Respect the signal for silence.
Speak English when you are asked to.
Do your homework on time.

Figure 16.3

Using classroom monitors

You can help keep good classroom control and discipline by making good use of student monitors. A monitor is a student who can help you with small but important and time-consuming jobs of classroom management such as:

► taking the register (by telling you who is absent);
► giving out and collecting homework;
► cleaning the blackboard;
► changing the class calendar date;
► opening and closing the window;
► helping the teacher with heavy loads;
► handing out activity cards/instructions to pairs or groups;
► marking reward stars on the wall chart.

You can appoint monitors on a rotation basis and it is a good idea to regularly change monitors to give everyone a chance. Being a monitor should be a positive and special role, so students will want to be a monitor and will do the job happily and well.

Signalling changes of activity easily and quickly

If we have planned variety into our lessons, then we change the activity quite often. We need to maintain classroom control and discipline when we move from one activity to another, so we need to teach and use clear signals to change activity easily and quickly. You can teach and practise a series of hand signals or pictures.

▶ To ask students to change the parts of a dialogue they are saying, make swapping gestures with your fingers, or show a card with a large double-ended arrow drawn on it.
▶ To tell students how long they have to complete the activity, show a card with a large '5' or '10' drawn on it (or the time you have planned) or draw a large '5' or '10' on the blackboard.
▶ To tell students that they have one minute left to finish the activity, show a card with a large '1' drawn on it, or draw a large '1' on the blackboard.

Achieving silence

There are times when you want the class to be silent, but students do not have to be silent all the time. School principals, other teachers and parents often think that a silent class is a good class where students are learning. However, a silent class does not necessarily mean that students are learning.

It is, however, very important for discipline and for learning that you can achieve and maintain silence quickly and easily when you want it. For example, it can be disturbing for some students to try to work with a background of other students talking, because it means that they cannot concentrate or hear the teacher.

You need to develop and practise simple and effective ways to achieve silence. For example, stand quietly with your arm held up, or gently tap the blackboard with a pencil for about ten seconds. Often, the most effective way to achieve silence is to be silent yourself. Shouting for silence does not usually work – it only encourages students to shout back. A teacher who does not shout encourages a quieter classroom.

With practice, your class will soon come to recognise these signs and will quieten down.

Maintaining discipline

However well you establish and maintain discipline in your class, sometimes things will go wrong. As we have seen, classroom discipline can be helped by agreeing classroom rules that everyone understands and keeps.

If problems start, you must take effective action before the situation gets worse. Do not let noise go on for long as it will become more of a challenge to stop it later. Use your technique for achieving silence. Find out if the students have finished their work, or if they do not understand what to do. In these situations, you can ask those who have finished early to work on the self-access materials and give extra help to those who have difficulties.

Sometimes, one or more students become bored or determined to make trouble. Then you have to prevent more discipline problems from happening. However, always be fair and apply the rules equally to all students. Be consistent in your use of rules, and take the same action for similar discipline challenges. Always be firm with your rules to stop bad behaviour, so that students understand exactly what will happen if they misbehave. Try to criticise the act rather than the student.

Some simple but effective ways to stop or limit discipline problems are to:

► ensure students enter, sit and leave the class in an orderly and quiet fashion, because if they start noisily, they will continue to be noisy;
► give students something to do as soon as they enter the classroom, such as writing down ten words beginning with the letter 'p'. This keeps students quiet and gives them some language revision before the lesson begins;
► tell students they will get a warning for unacceptable behaviour, but you must act next time;
► give as much encouraging praise as possible, especially to the weaker students and to students making an effort, and students who lack confidence;
► reward improvement, even if it is minimal, by giving stars that the student can display on a wall chart;
► select, or have a vote for, a 'student of the month' rewarded for continuous good effort and improving work, not just to the fast and clever students;
► show that you enjoy teaching, and helping students enjoy learning.

> **Classroom Action Task**
>
> Write out ideas for some classroom rules that you will discuss and agree with your students.

RECORDING PROGRESS

It is important to record your students' marks to keep track of the progress of the class. An up-to-date set of marks should be set out clearly and neatly in a mark book to give a realistic picture of individual students.

We need to record:

▶ who was absent, and when;
▶ who did the homework on time each time it was set;
▶ what marks you gave;
▶ test and exam marks;
▶ how well the class did the homework each time, as low marks from most of the class probably means that you did not teach it well.

Try to record marks and any comments immediately, because we easily forget. Make record-keeping part of your marking routine. Keeping a record of students' marks also helps in lesson planning, because we can see which activities our students found difficult and which they found easy, so that we can plan future lessons better.

We will look at specific practical ways to help you mark your students' work in the next chapter, but here we cover some different techniques of keeping a record of your students' learning and progress.

Continuous assessment

Continuous assessment is a way of monitoring the progress of students during the year. It helps teachers and students to identify their strengths and weaknesses as they learn and to improve those areas before the end-of-term test or the exam. If you wait for an end-of-term test, it may be too late to help your students.

You can do continuous assessment by recording:

▶ which students usually find the lessons the most challenging;
▶ what parts of each lesson appear to be more of a challenge to most of the class;
▶ which specific areas of language students find the most challenging.

You can make continuous assessment a part of a supportive learning atmosphere, so that your students are not afraid of what you are noting down. At first, your students will wonder what you are doing, so be open with them and explain it is to help you help them, but in a non-threatening way. If you do not name individual students, you can use this continuous assessment in class by saying:

'Some of you need a bit more help with . . . ', or
'I think this lesson needs a bit more practice.'

Student self-evaluation

All students need to know what they are good at and what they find more of a challenge. Self-evaluation is a challenging but rewarding process, and it can be discussed in class or kept private. We can teach students how to self-evaluate, and students get better at it with practice. You can encourage weak students to think of something good about themselves, and encourage stronger students to look for their weak areas.

You can help students start to evaluate themselves by asking them to try and answer the following questions. Write them on the blackboard for them to copy out and then fill in:

This week we studied ....
I learned ....
I found these things difficult: ....
I need more practice in: ....

Plan some time at the end of lessons (about five minutes is enough) to encourage students to think about their learning. Students can do this in a variety of ways. They can:

► keep this information secret;
► hand it in to you;
► compare with a partner;
► tell the teacher and the class.

Students may find this a bit of a challenge at first, but they will quickly learn, and you will learn a lot from their replies. Also, do not worry if students appear to have learned different things from the lesson: students learn in different ways.

17/ Ideas for Good Classroom Management

In the last chapter, we looked at planning lessons and organising students in the classroom. In this chapter we shall look at some more classroom management techniques. These techniques are always important, but good classroom management is particularly important in a large class.

TEACHER TALK

Teaching means giving information, so some teachers talk a lot in language learning lessons. This is because teachers have the facts and they need to pass this knowledge of language to their students. If you have a large class and few resources, it sometimes seems that the easiest way to teach is to stand at the front of the class and talk to the students. It may appear that this is the best way of using limited lesson time, and it may also appear to be the best option if you have only one or only very few textbooks.

But as we have said before, language learning is not just about knowing the rules, it is about being able to *use* language to communicate. If the teacher presents all material by talking, the students will not learn to communicate well. Even with a large class, there are many ways of planning your lessons so that your students have time to practise too.

Balancing teacher-talking time and student-talking time

One of the best ways to learn to communicate is to speak a lot; students therefore need plenty of speaking practice. The teacher already knows more English than the students, so teachers must learn to talk less in class and to plan how and when students can have more speaking practice. However, teachers need to talk for specific reasons, which include:

► greeting students;
► talking to students at the beginning and end of lessons;

- ► explaining new language;
- ► modelling new language;
- ► instructing students how to do an activity;
- ► indicating change of activity within a lesson;
- ► correcting mistakes.

Remember that the teacher has information to give to his or her students. So do not forget to say, clearly and simply at the beginning, the objectives of the lesson. Always mark changes of direction and summarise as the lesson continues. Ask students for the key points and write them on the blackboard.

Reading is a useful way of learning, so do not forget to back up explanations on the blackboard (see Chapter 19 for ideas on using the blackboard). Finally, near the end of the lesson tell students what they have learned. Ask them what they have learned, dealing with any misunderstandings or questions.

These procedures can help your teacher-talk become an effective part of your teaching, particularly if you are not very secure in your use of English, and your students are not very secure in their understanding of English.

Teachers' insecurity with English

According to the Direct Method, English language classes should be always taught in English. However, some teachers feel insecure about their own level of English. There are several reasons for this insecurity. Sometimes teachers:

- ► do not understand or use much English themselves;
- ► have never communicated with another English speaker;
- ► do not have enough training, qualifications or teaching experience;
- ► are more used to teaching English through their first language.

But by careful study, lesson planning, and practising your own English in every possible way, you will become more confident and your English will improve. You can:

- ► listen to English on the radio, television, videos and cassettes;
- ► read anything you find that is in English;
- ► use a bilingual dictionary to learn new words;
- ► write down any new words around you;
- ► regularly study a grammar book.

Giving clear instructions

You can introduce effective routines that can help to make you more confident with English, and to help students' confidence in understanding English.

▶ Use simple, short and clear English phrases as often as possible, especially when you are telling students what to do.

▶ Translate these phrases at first, if necessary, or write them on the blackboard.

▶ Use the gestures only, when the class becomes familiar with the gestures that you have taught them.

▶ Use the blackboard to reinforce spoken instructions, as it is visual and more permanent than spoken words. The instructions for an activity can be written on the blackboard as a constant reminder. This also saves the teacher constantly repeating instructions to students who are not listening or who do not understand.

▶ Make sure that all instructions are 'doubled': either in English followed, if possible, by a translation in the first language, or spoken in English with an explanatory gesture or with written instructions on the blackboard. To reinforce spoken instructions in non-spoken ways, you can say:

- 'Close your books'; at the same time you hold out the palms of your hands like a book, and then close them together.
- 'Listen', while putting your hand around your ear, to encourage students to listen carefully to what you are going to say.
- 'Together', while holding your arms at your side and then raising them and bringing them together at the front when you want the class to speak in chorus.

Figure 17.1

Reasons for using the students' first language in the classroom

In a monolingual class, where the teacher and students all speak a common language, it can be a challenge to keep everyone speaking in English. However, there are some good reasons for using the students' first or main language.

One good reason to use the first or main language is with low-level students, when some explanation or translation can help to reassure students that they understand. However, do not get into the habit of always explaining and translating everything, as then the students will learn to expect this. It can be a good idea to translate the new language when it is first presented to the class; however, by the Practice phase of the lesson, students should know the meaning.

You can use the students' first or main language to be absolutely sure that everyone understands (or ask students to translate for each other if you have a multilingual class). It is a good idea to say the words in English first, before the translation into the first language. If the students hear their own language first, they may not listen to the English translation which follows. At the same time, make sure you have a range of common and useful classroom phrases that you and your students understand and use. This is a simple and effective way to encourage and make the best use of English in the classroom.

Another good reason to use the first language is with high-level students. Often, at the higher levels of language learning, you will find single words or ideas or concepts in English or your language that either cannot be easily translated, or do not exist. In these cases it is much simpler and quicker to just give the word or phrase in your language.

Using consistent language

To help both teacher and students, it helps if you consistently use short and simple English phrases with your students. Teach these phrases to the class, write them on a wall chart, translate them if necessary. You can then expect students to understand and use these phrases themselves. Here are some possible phrases to regularly use with your class:

▶ Greeting students: 'Hello'; 'How are you?'.
▶ Chatting to students: 'What did you do at the weekend/last night?'.
▶ Telling students what they are going to do: 'Today we are going to learn how to . . .'.
▶ Asking the students to do something: 'Could you close the door?'.
▶ Instructing students: 'Look at the blackboard' 'Turn to page 5'.
▶ Asking students to repeat: 'Repeat after me'; 'Again'.

▶ Encouraging students to ask: 'What does . . . mean?'; 'What's the English for . . . ?'.

▶ Correcting students: 'Almost right'; 'Yes, but . . .'.

▶ Encouraging students to correct themselves: 'Try again'; ' Can you say that differently?'.

▶ Asking students to correct each other: ' Is he/she correct ?'; 'Is that right?'.

▶ Praising students: 'Good'; 'Well done'.

▶ Keeping discipline: 'Be quiet please'.

Questioning techniques

Teachers always expect to ask questions and students always expect to answer questions. Here are some ways of questioning which will help the students understand and speak English more easily.

Part of the teacher's work is to check understanding. Asking 'Do you understand?' is not a good question, as students will probably reply 'Yes'. Students sometimes do this because they do not want to annoy the teacher or they are worried about appearing slow. These feelings are understandable, but they are not very useful to the teacher or the students. Try to ask questions which check students' real understanding. There are three basic ways of asking a question.

Closed questions

Teachers ask students a lot of 'Yes/No' questions. This is possibly because it is the easiest way for the teacher to quickly understand the student's response. For example, part of a text could say:

'The man climbed slowly out of the boat at midnight, and walked carefully up the beach to the hut under the trees . . .'

The easy 'Yes/no' question is:

'Did the man climb slowly out of the boat at midnight?'

It is easy to answer because the student only has to match the words of the question to the words in the text, possibly without understanding, and then answer 'Yes' or 'No'.

Another easy questioning technique is to give students a choice of two answers. For example:

'Did the man walk slowly or quickly up the beach?'

This expects the answer 'He walked slowly' (because it is difficult to walk quickly and carefully).

If the text is difficult for the students, or you want to help students feel confident by getting questions correct, these questioning techniques are good.

Open questions

A more helpful but more challenging questioning technique is to ask open questions. They usually start with 'What . . .', 'When . . .', 'Why . . .', 'Who . . .', 'How . . . ' and there may be several possible correct answers to open questions. These questions test the students' understanding. For example, again using the above sample text sentence, the teacher can ask:

'Why did the man climb slowly out of the boat?'

Possible answers which show some understanding of the situation and the language can include:

'He was old' or 'He was hurt' or 'He was trying not to be seen or heard'.

Elicitation

Elicitation is when the teacher asks a series of simple questions that lead the students towards finding the answer for themselves. This often involves asking the students to use their imagination or transferring their feelings to the situation. Sometimes it would be easier and quicker to just tell the students the information, but training yourself and your students to think for themselves is a valuable teaching and learning technique. For example:

'What do you think the old man was feeling?', or you could ask
'What would you do in the same situation, if you were that old man?'
You can then ask 'Why do you think this?' and the students have to think of a logical answer.

You can do another form of elicitation with lower-level students using a picture to get suggestions from students about the characters and the situation or story in the picture, or pictures.

You ask 'Who can you see?', 'What are they doing?' in a series of linked questions to give students the chance to contribute their own ideas, and contribute to the learning process. (See Chapter 19 for more ideas about elicitation using the blackboard.)

> **Classroom Action Task**
>
> Think of a list of short and simple classroom instructions to use with your students. Write them on a large sheet of paper and put it up in your class where you and your students can see them, and make sure that you use them as much as possible.

MANAGING CLASSES WITH MIXED ABILITIES

Now let's look at one of the main challenges of a large class – a wide range of mixed abilities. Students in every class have:

- ▶ different language levels;
- ▶ different language learning skills;
- ▶ different learning speeds;
- ▶ different interests;
- ▶ different levels of confidence.

Some classes may also have a wide range of ages, so all classes are mixed ability, but the challenges are bigger in a large class. For example, weaker students may stop learning because they do not understand. The strong students sometimes dominate by gaining most of the teacher's attention and by giving all the answers. Sometimes the stronger ones stop learning because they find the work too easy and get bored. It is a big challenge to the teacher of a large class to help the weaker students and to keep the stronger students motivated so that all students succeed.

One way is to regularly move students around. You can do this by asking students to move around, for example to move forward one row each month. This means that they all get a regular chance of sitting in the front row, which gives students the best chance of feeling involved and of receiving maximum attention and help from the teacher.

If you have a wide range of ages in your class, this may be less suitable because the older students may be taller than the younger students, and so the shorter students will need to be in front of the taller students. But whatever your classroom situation, you can work out a way of moving students so that different students have the chance of working with each other during the term.

Moving students around has other advantages too: it helps classroom discipline by preventing small groups, which may become disruptive, from forming. It also means that students of different abilities work together, rather than always having the stronger students in one row or group, and the weaker ones in another.

The teacher's attitude towards a large class of mixed ability students can also have a good or bad effect on their attitudes to and successes in learning. If you use negative words like 'lazy' or 'stupid' to students who may not appear to be the fastest or best students in your class, you may have long-term problems with motivation and discipline.

So we need to think about the techniques, materials and activities we will use in order to manage the stronger students, average students and weaker students.

Dealing with weak, average and stronger students

We can plan learning activities where the *weaker* students can complete only one part. It is better to finish part of the work easily and correctly, than to complete all the work in a hurry or incorrectly.

The *average* students can finish the whole learning activity.

The *stronger* students can complete all the planned learning activity, and in addition they can be given some extra questions or examples to do. Another way to ensure that the stronger students do not waste their learning time is to encourage them to work by themselves. We call this self-access learning.

Teachers can also use the individual differences and use the range of skills, abilities and personalities in the class to everyone's advantage. One way of making it easier to distribute your time is to ask students to work in groups, according to their different abilities.

To help the slower, weaker or less confident students you need to give these students more time to help them understand and be successful. It is more of a challenge in a large class, so all the more important. The average and fast or strong students will need less of your time, so you can spend most time with students who need you most.

If you call the groups A, B, C and D, or 1, 2, 3 and 4, it will be clear who is top of the class and who is bottom. Most students know how good they are, and realise who the weaker or slower students are, so neutral group names are more positive. Call the groups, for example, 'the Lions', 'the Tigers', 'the Giraffes' and 'the Leopards', or the 'Red/Blue/Green/Yellow' groups.

You can give more time to the students who need more of your attention if you form separate groups of weak, average and strong students. To help the weak students, you can do some remedial work and give careful correction. At the same time, you need not ignore the students in the average and strong groups, but help them when they ask you.

Another way of forming groups which can help with different learning abilities is to put students in mixed ability groups. In these groups you can encourage the stronger students to help the weaker ones. If you encourage this peer teaching, or 'pair helping', as a positive thing to do, usually most of the stronger students are keen to take on this role.

You will find more activities on organising and managing group and pair work in Chapter 18.

Self-access materials are not difficult or time-consuming to make. You could have a special self-access box in the corner of the room. In this box, students can find or make word games; for example, 'How many words can you make using the letters of the word "discipline"?'. Or there could be an English reading text for which the students have to make up questions for another student to answer. The idea is to keep all the class busy, interested in learning and quiet, and this is particularly important with a large class (Figure 17.2).

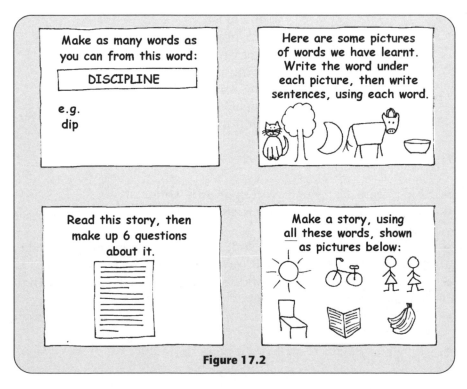

Figure 17.2

CORRECTION AND MARKING

There are some disadvantages of marking and correcting every mistake. This is because marking:

► can take a long time;
► can be demotivating if a student's work is covered with red marks;
► is not always a good learning process, because students do not usually look at the corrections in detail.

As we mentioned in teaching 'process' writing (in Chapter 11), you can teach your students a correction code. Knowing this code prevents students relying on the teacher to correct everything and saves the teacher time in correcting every mistake.

Correction techniques should always work towards students correcting themselves or other students. They may have to do this when they no longer have English lessons and have to write without support and correction from a teacher. So you must teach them how to do this. You can teach any code that you think is suitable.

Here is an example, which was first introduced on page 76:

T	=	wrong tense
G	=	wrong grammar
W	=	wrong word,
^	=	missing word(s)
WO	=	wrong word order
S	=	wrong spelling
?	=	I don't understand

How to use a correction code:

► First, students try to correct their own work.
► Then try 'pair helping', where students try to find and correct each other's mistakes.
► Next, you collect the work, and, without correcting every mistake, guide students towards their mistakes using a correction code.
► Give the code-corrected work back to the students and ask them to try and work out their mistakes.
► Encourage students to correct their own mistakes, and to help each other.
► Finally, students re-write their work to produce a correct version.

Correcting work this way can take extra time, especially when you and your students are trying out this new marking process. However, it is part of the learning process and students are learning from their mistakes, and they will make fewer mistakes in future pieces of writing. So a little extra work can help in the long term.

You can also try underlining mistakes and suggesting the type of mistake, so the students have to think for themselves, particularly in an exam. Correcting written work with a code helps students in these ways because it motivates them to think about what they have written, and it helps them learn from their mistakes.

MARKING AND SELF-EVALUATING

Marking is very important and we can make marking quicker and easier, which is good for both teachers and students. Some teachers spend a lot of time marking students' work, but students find that there is not enough time to ask the teacher about any mistakes in their homework. So there need to be other ways to deal with homework, and a little time needs to be planned into the lesson for students to ask about their homework.

Checking work in class through homework

One way of checking work done in class is by giving homework. Written homework can be a follow-up activity to a lesson, but sometimes students make mistakes or maybe they do not complete the homework. Perhaps the problem is that the homework was too difficult or too long. Here are some ideas to help make homework easier to do and easier to mark:

▶ Give homework regularly, so that students know when to expect it and they receive regular reinforcement of work done in class.
▶ Tell students when you want the homework given in. Do not accept late homework.
▶ Negotiate with other teachers when to give homework, so that the students do not get overloaded on certain days.
▶ Keep homework *short* and *easy* so that students will do it, and it is easier to mark, so that students will do it successfully.
▶ Teach students a marking code, so that you do not always have to write all the correct answers in all the students' homework.

How to make marking easier:

▶ Mark as soon as possible after you receive homework, or the pile of work will quickly become a mountain.
▶ Mark some books every day, and even-out this work over a week.
▶ If you have large class, you can decide to only mark half of the homework books each time and to mark the other half next time. Do not tell the students until afterwards, or they may not do the homework!
▶ Mark fairly, positively and helpfully.
▶ Use a consistent marking system.
▶ Make it clear what you are marking the homework for – is it for grammar, content, style, effort or presentation, and give a separate mark for each aspect of the homework.

Using a basic list of comments

A comment is more helpful than just a grade or a number out of ten.

▶ Be positive, but truthful and encouraging – 'Good, but . . . '; 'Better than last week'.
▶ Indicate how the student can improve – 'Check spellings in a dictionary first'; 'Keep your sentences short, no more than sixteen words'; 'Make sure you have a beginning and an end to your story', 'Make sure the verb in each sentence agrees with the subject of the sentence'.
▶ Remember – 'Must do better' is not a helpful comment.
▶ Encourage students to re-write corrections, to help them learn from their mistakes.

Marking written work in class:

▶ Ask class monitors to write the correct answers on the blackboard or to read them out.
▶ Ask students to swap their written work before doing this kind of correction.
▶ Write students' mistakes on the blackboard (but do not name the students who made the mistakes), and ask all the class to correct all the mistakes.

18/ Pair and Group Work

In this chapter we will look at group and pair work in more detail, including how to organise it and manage it. Pair and group work allows all students to practise language and to actively participate. That is why pair and group work are important techniques to use in large classes, where otherwise only a few stronger or more confident students have the opportunity to participate.

MAKING THE BEST USE OF PAIR WORK AND GROUP WORK

Pair work and group work involves the whole class working separately in pairs or small groups at the same time.

Pair and group work is important because it:

▶ gives students lots of practice in using a language;
▶ allows the quieter students to speak to a partner, instead of speaking in front of the whole class;
▶ teaches students to help each other with their learning.

Pair work and group work may be a new teaching and learning technique for you and your students. Some people may think that pair and group work is not 'real' learning, and it is true that it can be noisy and time-consuming.

However, pair and group work is a very good way to manage large classes with mixed abilities and it can improve motivation and students' use of English. The teacher does not give up control during pair or group work, but controls the whole class differently. The teacher has no loss of authority, and, if carefully managed and monitored, this additional way of learning can help all your students.

In a large class, pair work and group work needs careful planning to keep all the students involved in the lesson and allow them to work with each other. Pair and group work gives all students lots of practice time.

Using these activities in the Practice and Production phases of a lesson allows students to talk about their own ideas, opinions and real-life facts. The aim of working together is to give students lots of practice and help so that they can develop real communication skills.

Larger groups can be more difficult to organise, so you can start with pair work. When your students and you can organise and work in pairs quickly and easily, you can go on to try a larger group work activity.

INTRODUCING PAIR AND GROUP WORK INTO TRADITIONAL CLASSROOMS

In many classrooms, group or pair work may be a new way of teaching and learning. If students are used to sitting in rows and listening to the teacher, then the idea of working in groups or pairs can seem intimidating. So, when you introduce pair work or group work for the first time, you need to explain to the students that, in one phase of the lesson, you will ask them to work with each other to practise new language they have recently learnt.

You need to explain that this type of activity is to help them to become more accurate and fluent in English, it is not a test. You will also need to give clear instructions on what you expect them to do and how you expect them to behave. Tell your students that all the class will be talking at the same time, so they must speak quietly. Be prepared to repeat instructions and to give lots of guidance to encourage students to get started and to complete the activity.

Choose a short and easy activity. Let your students work in pairs first, then go on to try working in groups of three to six. Remember to present the new language to the whole class before giving the students a chance to work with each other.

Pair work language practice can be a two- to six-line dialogue, in the form of questions and answers, using the grammar and vocabulary you have recently presented. A simple two-line question and answer dialogue for the grammar 'Have you got any . . . ?', with student 'A' asking student 'B', would be:

A: 'Have you got any brothers?' 'B' has a choice of reply:
B: 'Yes, I've got (two)' or ' No I haven't'.

First you need to explain who will take the 'A' part and who will take the 'B' part of the dialogue. It can help prevent confusion if you also write these instructions on the blackboard.

Demonstrate the speaking activity with a confident student, then repeat it with a pair of students standing at the front. This will show everyone what you expect them to do.

Next, organise the whole class into pairs. The first few times you do pair work, you need to say who will work together. You quickly name the pairs by either indicating the pairs, or by showing with your hands who will work together. After a few lessons, you can tell the class to turn to a partner beside them. In later lessons, you can ask the students to pair up with someone in front of them or behind them. These varieties of pairings ensure that all students work with at least four different partners over a period of time, and gives them all a change of working styles and learning experiences. The students will soon get used to pairing up quickly and quietly. If your students sit in rows of seats or benches fixed to the floor, and there are odd numbers in a row, ask some students to work in a line of three.

When the pairs have been set up, and everyone knows what to do, start the pair work activity with an agreed signal. You could raise your arm or wave your hand. You also need a signal to stop the activity; for

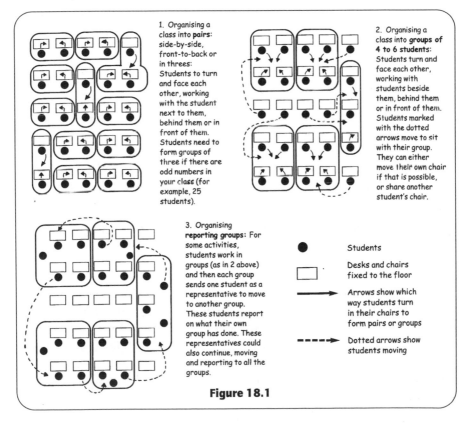

1. Organising a class into **pairs**: side-by-side, front-to-back or in threes: Students to turn and face each other, working with the student next to them, behind them or in front of them. Students need to form groups of three if there are odd numbers in your class (for example, 25 students).

2. Organising a class into **groups of 4 to 6 students**: Students turn and face each other, working with students beside them, behind them or in front of them. Students marked with the dotted arrows move to sit with their group. They can either move their own chair if that is possible, or share another student's chair.

3. Organising **reporting groups**: For some activities, students work in groups (as in 2 above) and then each group sends one student as a representative to move to another group. These students report on what their own group has done. These representatives could also continue, moving and reporting to all the groups.

●　　Students

▭　　Desks and chairs fixed to the floor

➡　　Arrows show which way students turn in their chairs to form pairs or groups

- - -➤　　Dotted arrows show students moving

Figure 18.1

example, tap the blackboard or your desk with a pencil or your fingers for about ten seconds, or until everyone has stopped.

When your students are learning how to work in pairs, keep the speaking short – four to five minutes is enough. Most importantly, leave the students alone to try out the language. If you use pair work for the production stage of a lesson, this is an opportunity for the students to practise without constant help or correction from the teacher.

Other examples of how you can use pair and group work are:

▶ You can cue language to prompt dialogue or conversations. You can show a card with a word or several words (but not complete sentences). You can also write these on the blackboard a word. These words can help students to make correct sentences. In pair work activities, you cue a question for one student in the pair, and the answer for the other student in the pair. Pictures can also help produce a spoken response. For example, if the question is 'What did you do yesterday?', the answer can be cued with a picture of a market/a cinema/a football pitch. There are more examples of drilling activities in Chapters 6 to 12.

▶ To make sure all students are involved, each pair or group could silently read a short text. Then, for the next stage, the group discusses the answers to questions together. Finally, everyone writes their own answers, and then within the group students check each other's answers. For variety, sometimes ask the students to give feedback in an indirect way. For example, write a letter or report about what they talked about, or give a spoken presentation from a reading or writing activity. (See Chapter 14 for more ideas on presentations.) The teacher only needs to offer help if asked to do so by the group. This kind of group work is collaborative, where the group effort, and especially the group discussion, helps everyone.

SUMMARISING THE INTRODUCTION OF PAIR AND GROUP WORK

▶ Explain to your students why pair and group work is a good idea.
▶ Present new language and practise it with the whole class first.
▶ Indicate the pairs or groups who will be working together.
▶ Demonstrate with a pair of students at the front of the class.
▶ Tell students to speak quietly if everyone will be talking at the same time.
▶ Tell students not to worry about making mistakes during the Production phase.

▶ Explain carefully what the students will have to do.

▶ Reinforce the instructions by writing them on the blackboard.

▶ Signal the start of the activity.

▶ Move away from the centre front of the classroom.

▶ Look, listen and take notes of common and difficult mistakes.

▶ Signal the end of the activity.

▶ Give or ask for appropriate feedback.

▶ Do a few minutes of pair work every lesson, until you and your students feel happy to try group work.

▶ Persist in doing pair and group work, even if you find it a challenging teaching technique, because it very effectively helps your students to use language.

RESPONSIBILITY WITHIN GROUPS

Teachers can encourage students to work well in groups by giving different students various roles and responsibilities. Having different roles within a group encourages students to do the activity properly and helps students to grow in confidence or develop different skills. Also, you know that you can rely on certain members of a group to do particular tasks, so management of the activity is easier.

Some group activities need different organisation. Perhaps a text needs to be given out, or a piece of work exchanged between groups. So it is very useful for the teacher and the students if one person in each group takes the role of 'monitor', who has responsibility for collecting and giving out work as required. This role should be regularly changed, so different students get a chance.

In a group activity that demands a lot of English to be used, it helps to have a 'secretary' and a 'leader' and maybe a 'presenter' and a 'monitor':

▶ The 'secretary' listens and takes brief notes on what is discussed or agreed. The role of 'secretary' can be given to a talkative student, who then has to concentrate on listening to the others in the group.

▶ The role of 'leader' can be given to a quiet or shy student, because this role gives them the chance to talk by having to ask other members of the group to speak. This role can also be given to confident students as it limits their speaking, and allows the quieter ones to speak.

▶ The role of 'presenter' can be given to a student who is confident in speaking, as this person will have to give the results of the group discussion to another group, but only after listening to what their group says. This role can also be given to quieter students to give them some specific speaking to do.

▶ The role of 'monitor' can be given to a student with the best level of English in the group, who checks that everyone is speaking English correctly. The role can also be given to a shy student, who can encourage everyone in the group to have a turn, and to make sure that only English is being used.

USE OF FIRST LANGUAGE IN GROUP WORK

If your class has a language in common, the students may use their first or main language instead of English during pair or group work. There are two approaches to this situation.

First, you can allow certain parts of a speaking activity to be done in the students' first language, for example, if the students are deciding who will do what or discussing a difficult idea. But the Production phrase of the activity must be done in English.

Second, if, during short, guided activities, students are using too much first language, you can encourage the use of English by gently telling, or jokingly asking, students to speak in English. You can remind them that this is their only opportunity to practise speaking English.

It is possible that your students are using too much first language because they are not certain of what they are supposed to do. So make sure they are well prepared, and that they understand what each person in the pair or group is supposed to do. You can reinforce your spoken instructions by writing them on the blackboard.

In large classes, some groups finish before other groups and then they might start chatting in their first language or possibly become disruptive. Make sure that you keep the activity short. Usually when about three-quarters of the class has finished, you can stop the activity. For the students who have not finished, make sure that you tell them that it does not matter. For those students who finish a short activity early, encourage them to chat quietly in English. In a longer activity direct them to self-access materials (for ideas on using self-access materials, see Chapter 16).

DEALING WITH THE NOISE PRODUCED BY PAIR AND GROUP WORK

During pair and group work, it is important to be able to distinguish between naughty noise and busy noise. Naughty noise is disruptive. It usually means that either the students do not understand what they have to do, or they have finished what you told them to do. In both cases they get bored and start talking loudly in their first language, and may start misbehaving. This situation means that you have not prepared or monitored the class well enough, or that the activity has gone on for too long.

However, even if you have prepared the group work well, there are situations that you will have to deal with. The students eagerly start speaking, but, with the general background of everyone else speaking, everyone speaks a little louder. On these occasions, simply tell the class, or particular groups, to speak more quietly. You may have to repeat this several times as the noise level builds up again, and you could try and develop a hand gesture which means 'Speak quietly'. Usually after a few sessions of pair or group work, students learn to keep their voices down, as they realise they are not in competition for the teacher's attention. Teach your students that when you raise your hand, they have to raise their hand and stop talking. This can help when it becomes a bit noisy, or in a large class where all the students may not be able to see the teacher, but they will soon see the raised hands and realise that they must be silent.

You may also get complaints from the class next to yours about the noise, and if the walls are thin, then even quiet talking will be disruptive to your neighbours. There are several ways to overcome this:

► Tell the teacher next door what you are going to do, and explain that this speaking activity will only take a few minutes.
► Plan and do the pair and group work when the next class is somewhere else.
► Wait until it rains and then do the speaking activity, as the noise of the rain will make the effect of the class speaking less obvious.
► Go outside to a far corner of the playground, where you will not disturb other students and have your speaking practice there.

MONITORING PAIR AND GROUP WORK

The teacher needs to have good classroom management skills to make sure that pair and group work activities do not get out of control. Here are some tips:

- ▶ First you carefully explain the work to be done, and set up the pairs or groups.
- ▶ Then you must make sure all the students know what to do, and check that they are all using English.
- ▶ Choose the pairs and groups, ensuring different pairing or grouping on a regular basis.
- ▶ Do not stay at the centre, in front of the class, because the students will keep looking at you, waiting for your reaction to their English.
- ▶ Move slowly around the class, if possible, or move to the side, back or middle of the class, but move away from the centre of the front, so that you are less noticeable.
- ▶ Walk around slowly and quietly, just looking and listening carefully, but try to avoid eye contact, to help the students realise you are not constantly going to correct and help them. Check that the students are speaking in English.
- ▶ Do not correct mistakes if it is the Production phase of a lesson, but note down any common problems or mistakes.
- ▶ Listen to the language used, and watch how the students are working together, but try not to get too close to the pairs or groups, or interfere with their attempts to communicate.
- ▶ Only help a pair or group if communication has broken down and they do not know what to say, or if someone asks you for help, or if they run out of ideas.
- ▶ Leave your students alone during the Production phase as this is an opportunity to practise the English they have learnt.
- ▶ Do feedback and correction afterwards.
- ▶ You are making the best use of student participation in the learning process, but you are still in control.

FEEDBACK AND CORRECTION OF GROUP AND PAIR WORK

The final stage of pair and group work is the feedback and correction stage. You do not always have to get everyone to say what they have talked about or agreed upon, but if you do feedback there are some points to think about:

▶ It can take a long time to get all the groups to do feedback, so you could think about asking one or two groups only. Next time, you can choose two different groups.

▶ Sometimes you can encourage competitiveness and fast working, by saying that the first group to finish the activity can write it on the blackboard or tell the class.

▶ Another form of feedback is to ask each group to choose a 'presenter' who will then each go to another group and tell the new group what their group did or decided.

▶ Maybe a pair of 'presenters' from each group can move around and demonstrate their dialogues to other groups.

▶ You can encourage the students to ask further questions at this stage, when the 'presenters' have to explain or defend their groups' work.

Correction of work done in pair or group work is important and it needs to be done in a way that does not pick out individuals, or they may be unwilling to speak in a pair or group next time. At the same time, you need to make sure that you help students with their language difficulties. Remember that during the Production phase of a speaking activity, you monitor their speaking practice by walking around and noting any common mistakes or language that causes a lot of difficulty.

You can do the correction by writing incorrect sentences that you heard on the blackboard, and then asking for the correct version. If any mistakes cause difficulties, then do a quick explanation and drilling exercise to revise the specific language. You could alternatively write each incorrect sentence on a separate piece of paper and hand them out randomly. The students could then try to write the sentence correctly. A good follow-up to this correction technique is to then swap the papers around, so that the students can check each other's corrections.

If you regularly organise short pair and group work learning activities, your class will soon become used to this additional learning style. The organisation will soon become easier and quicker, as everyone knows what to do.

Classroom Action Task

Look at the lessons you are teaching next week.

Find a suitable point in each lesson, where two to three minutes of pair work could be planned, making sure it is after new language has been presented to and practised by the whole class.

Plan carefully how you will organise the activity.

Do the pair work activity in class.

After the class has finished, note in your Teacher's Action Diary what you think about how the pair work went, what went well and what did not go very well, and why.

Do not expect pair work to go smoothly the first time you and your class do it, because this learning style takes a bit of practice.

Next time you do pair work, remember what did not go so well last time, and try to improve.

When you feel confident with pair work, try a short, well-planned group work activity next, following the same learning process as you did for pair work.

19/ Using the Blackboard

In this chapter we look at how resources can motivate students, and start by giving a range of activities for using the most common classroom resource – the blackboard.

USING RESOURCES TO IMPROVE MOTIVATION AND PARTICIPATION

Resources are books, any person, animal, plant or any object that makes teaching and learning easier, clearer and more interesting. Students need to be motivated, because learning is a long and sometimes difficult process. So how can we use resources to motivate students and improve their learning?

Seeing, touching and smelling real objects (or drawings or photos if you cannot find the real object, or if the real object is too big or too expensive), is very motivating. Telling a story, describing something or someone, or practising a dialogue is more memorable with an object or picture in front of you.

In many classes, the blackboard is the only teaching aid. It is also the teaching aid which most teachers are most familiar with. We need to use the blackboard often and in the most efficient way. This is why we will spend the rest of this chapter looking at how we can use the blackboard.

HOW TO USE THE BLACKBOARD

In a large class with few resources, the blackboard is the most useful teaching and learning aid. Students learn better with more written and visual help from the blackboard, so we need to think about how you can use the blackboard.

You can use the blackboard for successful learning in several different ways. It can be used to:

► give a visual context for presenting language (for example, drawing pictures);
► record spellings;
► present word order and sentence structure;
► explain grammar points;
► show grammar variations in sentences clearly;
► give non-spoken cues for further practice in writing and speaking;
► be a source of text for students without books.

Usually the blackboard is used only for writing, but pictures of people, objects and scenes add variety, and they are easy to do with a little practice. With either words or pictures, you should follow these guidelines.

► Make drawings or pictures clear and large so that students at the back of the class can see easily.
► Do not stand in front of what you are writing or drawing, so either write standing with your side to the blackboard, or frequently move to one side.
► Ask students as you write 'What word is next?' or 'Is this the correct spelling?'.
► Ask students as you draw ''Who is this?' or 'Where is he?' or 'What is he doing?'.

An important teaching skill is to be able to draw people, objects and scenes quickly, easily and effectively. Anyone can learn the basics of drawing. If your drawings are a bit odd at first, don't worry, it is not a problem. If students laugh at your drawings, at least they will remember them. Language learning with pictures can help by:

► helping students who like to learn with an emphasis on pictures and charts;
► making meanings clearer, and helping to prevent misunderstandings;
► discouraging students from translating from their first language.

Figure 19.1 depicts some drawings for you to practise.

Figure 19.1

Classroom Action Task	Choose the drawings above that will be useful to you and practise doing them.
	Copy them until you feel confident.
	Next close the book and try to remember the drawings, and draw them quickly.
	Finally practise the drawings on your blackboard, and use some in your lessons.
	Remember: all your classroom pictures must be simple and quickly drawn.

PLANNING HOW TO USE THE BLACKBOARD

When you are planning each lesson you need to think about where everything will fit on the blackboard. Begin by thinking about how you will use the blackboard at different stages of the lesson and how the blackboard will look at the end of the lesson. Things to think about are how to:

▶ give a visual context for new language (for example, drawing pictures);
▶ explain and record new language clearly;
▶ place sentences for copying by students;
▶ use pictures and charts effectively;
▶ make sure certain areas can be erased to make space for later additions;
▶ note homework;
▶ deal with unexpected items.

Classroom Action Task

Look at the sample blackboard in Figure 19.2. How could you improve the organisation?

Re-draw the blackboard, dividing it into areas for words, grammar and any extras.

You can find one possible redrawn blackboard at the end of this chapter.

Figure 19.2

You can use the blackboard to help present and practise new language more clearly than with just an explanation from the teacher. The information can be given in words, pictures and charts to make understanding easier. You can use the blackboard to show similarities, patterns and the differences between structures.

You can help to explain the grammatical form of new language by:

▶ underlining, circling and boxing letters or words;
▶ using different coloured chalks to emphasise or categorise sets of words or grammar structures;
▶ using arrows to show how the order of words can change (see Figure 7.3).

You can help students practise new language by making charts, substitution tables, or diagrams.

USING DRAWINGS ON THE BLACKBOARD

We have made a lot of suggestions, throughout this book, on how to use blackboard drawings. Here are some ideas for using drawings on the board to present and practise language.

The Presentation phase

You can draw objects, alone or in combination, to explain the meaning of new words or to establish a situation in which a new grammatical structure is used. Gradually build up the picture or the scene, while constantly asking students 'What is this?', 'Who is this?'. For example, a circle could be the beginning of a ball, an orange, a head or a globe. By slowly adding detail and stopping to ask students what they think you are drawing, they remain involved, interested and use more English.

The Practice phase

Blackboard drawings are excellent as cues for drilling. First, draw and elicit the meanings of some cue words in the sentences you want to drill and then point to them as you drill. For example, draw examples of fruit on the board and drill 'Have you got any bananas/guavas/melons/lemons/?'. 'Yes, I have/No, I haven't.' In substitution tables, you can draw pictures instead of writing words, for example for practising likes and dislikes. Using pictures makes the activity a little more challenging, because the students have to know the words for the pictures and do not simply read the words off the blackboard.

USING CHARTS

Charts made on the blackboard are easy to set up. They are a very useful way to help students actively participate in the lesson by practising and creating different kinds of sentences, without mistakes. Charts can be used at any stage of the lesson, and they can be used to present and practise almost anything.

Does	he she Peter Iman	like	oranges? bananas? peaches? milk? fish?

Figure 19.3

Figure 19.3 gives the maximum help to the students, while allowing some word choice. If they choose one word from each column, their sentence will be correct. For example: 'Does Iman like oranges?' or 'Does he like peaches?'. All combinations are correct.

Do Does	you they she he Shiv Alia	like	oranges? bananas? peaches? milk? fish?

Figure 19.4

Figure 19.4 is still very guided, but there is a choice to be made with 'Do/Does . . . ?'. For example: 'Does Jan like oranges?' or 'Do they like oranges?'.

These two charts show small variations in a question using 'Do/Does . . . ?'. You can use this question-forming activity later in a lesson as the basis of a class questionnaire. The food items can be suggested by the class, or by individual groups. Then groups of four to six students ask each other the questions from the chart.

After practising the question until the students are confident and fluent with the whole structure, another form of this chart can help with the answers.

Yes	he we you I	don't does
No	she they	doesn't do

Figure 19.5

Using the columns in Figure 19.5 leads to the four possible types of response:

'Yes, he does/No, he doesn't/Yes, they do/No, they don't'. The language used and the information discovered can be presented and practised in a different way, with a different kind of chart. Here only subject and object words are used, such as Jan and Iman, and bananas/fish/oranges/milk.

To give extra practice in remembering the vocabulary of food items, the words can be replaced with a picture. There are no cues for the correct structure, so the students use the given information as a basis for their sentences.

Like and dislike chart

	bananas	fish	oranges	milk
Jan	X	X	X	✓
Iman	✓	X	✓	✓

Figure 19.6

Students ask their classmates questions like: 'Do you like bananas?'. If the answer is 'Yes', a tick is put next to that person's name. If the answer is 'No', put a cross next to their name. Each student or group fills in their chart by asking other students the same question and noting the responses with a tick or cross.

It is usually better to use symbols instead of writing full answers, which take time and could contain errors. These activities encourage lots of speaking practice for all the students in the class. They have something to talk about and the guided practice prevents them making mistakes.

When students have all this information they can do a follow-up speaking and/or writing activity. They can tell each other, or write about their friends' likes and dislikes, or do a class survey. The language used will include:

'Jan doesn't like bananas (but he likes milk)' or
'Iman likes bananas and oranges' or
'Jan and Iman like milk (but they don't like fish)'

With a different class or later in the term, you can use this same information to practise more difficult grammar structures, for example: 'Neither Jan nor Iman like fish (but they both like rice)'. This idea could be extended by using the concept of a tick for a positive answer, and a cross for a negative answer. Two ticks for an answer could mean to like very much or to love something, and two crosses could mean to hate or can't stand something.

Strong likes and dislikes chart

	bananas	fish	oranges	milk
Ebou	✓	✓✓	X	XX
Elsa	X	XX	✓	XX

Figure 19.7

Possible language made from this chart could include:

'Ebou loves fish but he can't stand milk' or
'Elsa hates both milk and fish'.

Tenses and time can also be presented and practised with a chart like the one in Figure 19.8. The words and numbers tell us about Shiv's daily routine.

Time and action chart

6.30	Get up
6.45	Have breakfast
7.00	Leave home
8.15	Start school

Figure 19.8

With this kind of chart, students can practise questions and answers like:

'What does Shiv do at six-thirty/half past six?' 'He gets up' or
'When does Shiv start school?' 'At eight-fifteen/quarter past eight'.

You can find these basic and useful structures in many textbooks. Sometimes the structure charts are included in the book. It is good for students to have a different way of learning and using language sometimes. You can ask the students to look at the blackboard instead of the book all the time. You can write any structures that are not given in the textbook on a chart similar to the examples illustrated above.

PUTTING TEXT ON THE BLACKBOARD

Sometimes the teacher has the only copy of the textbook, but students may also need to have their own copy of the text, part of the text, or at least to have key information in their own notebooks. You can use the blackboard in an effective way to make sure that they have this, to keep them involved and interested. As they take in and understand the information, they can also practise language by carrying out writing, speaking, listening and reading activities which are based on the text. This way of learning is more useful than spending a lot of time simply copying from the blackboard.

First, if you have a long text, think about how you can shorten this by summarising it, or by preparing key sentences from the story or about the information. You can also prepare a simpler version of any pictures or diagrams which are in your copy of the text, for you to use on the blackboard during the lesson.

Begin by dividing the blackboard into three sections. The first section is for pictures, the second for practice activities and the third for the edited text or key sentences. Let's now look at how you can use pictures to revise and check vocabulary, and to illustrate the main points of the situation of the story. You can do this by drawing a guided series of step-by-step pictures about the text in the first section of the blackboard. Draw only a small part at a time, asking your students a series of questions as you draw:

Who . . . / What . . . / When . . . / How . . . / Why . . . ? questions.

You can teach or check important vocabulary and encourage your students to talk about the information in the text in a simple but logical way. Every important part of the story or situation is picked out in a simple drawing, and a relevant question is asked.

Look at the drawings below (Figure 19.9). On page 151 you can see what the teacher asks students as he or she draws the pictures on the first section of the blackboard.

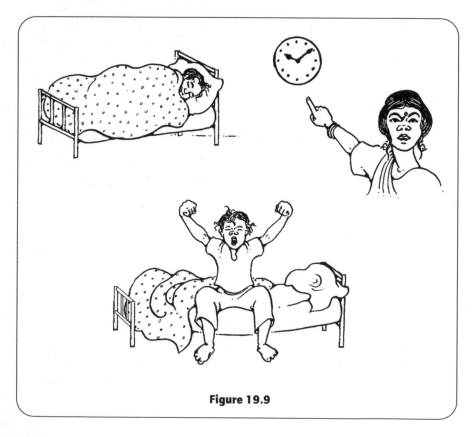

Figure 19.9

'Who's this?'
'What's he doing?'
'What's the time?'
'Who's she?'
'What's she saying?'
'Why's she saying this?'
'How is he feeling now?
'What might happen next?'

Guided questions and answers like these will lead the students through the information in the whole text (or your summary or key points), and prepare them for some writing or speaking activities about it.

Now that students know the information fairly well, you can begin to put some text on the blackboard by asking further questions. Leave the pictures on the blackboard as a reminder and put the reading or writing exercises on the second section of the blackboard.

Here are some useful types of exercises to do when you feel your students know the information fairly well.

Gap-filling sentences

When students have suggested some correct sentences and written them on the blackboard, go back and rub out some of the words, drawing a line to mark each missing word. You could rub out all the verbs, all the prepositions, vocabulary items or important words from the text. To make this easier, you could write the missing words, in jumbled order, under the sentences.

Matching half-sentences

As the students suggest a sentence, the teacher writes one half of it in a left-hand column, and the second half of the sentence in a right-hand column, but not opposite. Later, students have to find, match and write complete correct sentences.

Re-ordering jumbled sentences

When students suggest sentences, write them on the blackboard in an incorrect order (for example, sentence 1 at the bottom of the black-board, sentence 2 in the middle of the blackboard, sentence 3 in between these two sentences, and sentence 4 at the top). Students then reconstruct the story by putting the sentences in the correct order. Students can read the correct version of these exercises either individually or in chorus, to give them some very simple reading practice.

You can also give students listening practice, which will reinforce the information in the text. Draw a chart on the blackboard which the students can quickly copy, and then read the text out to them in manageable sections, so that they are not overloaded with information. While you read the text, the students fill in their chart with ticks or crosses as they listen, to note their understanding of what they hear. Then the students can discuss and check the information they recorded on the chart, in pairs or groups, and preferably in English. This activity also gives them speaking practice using the vocabulary of the text, as well as checking the information again.

PUTTING A LONGER TEXT ON THE BLACKBOARD BY A CLASS RECONSTRUCTION ACTIVITY

Advanced students and other students who need to have a longer text in their own notebooks may not need to do all the detailed language practice outlined above. However, a listening activity, such as filling in key points on a chart and then discussing them, will help students recall the information.

It is still necessary to do some 'before-reading' activities (see Chapter 9) before you read the complete text (or your summary or key sentences) to them. Next you can read again the first part of the text and use open questions (Who/What/When/Why/Where/How) to check their understanding. As you hear correct sentences, write them on the blackboard using the third section of your divided blackboard. After two or three sentences, tell students to copy them into their notebooks. Repeat this procedure until they have copied all the necessary text from their suggested sentences from the blackboard. As you can see, this way of asking for and using suggestions from students, questioning and copying keeps the students involved in the whole process, as well as reinforcing the information that they need to know.

LETTING THE STUDENTS USE THE BLACKBOARD

So far we have talked about how the teacher can use the blackboard. But many of these activities can be done by the students. It is important to allow your students some blackboard participation. This is for several reasons:

▶ If students feel they are an active part of the lesson, they will be more motivated to learn.

▶ Students are usually happy to compete for a turn to write or draw on the board, and it is fun for them to check each other's suggestions on the blackboard.

▶ Students who watch their classmates writing on the blackboard look carefully for mistakes, and they can easily be encouraged to correct and offer alternatives.

And finally, here is a reminder of the important points to remember when using the blackboard as a public arena:

▶ The blackboard can be useful at all stages of the lesson.

▶ You can get the important parts of the textbook onto the blackboard, if there is only one or few textbooks available.

▶ Drawings are as useful as words, and with a little practice everyone can do simple, quick and effective drawings.

▶ Effective blackboard planning can motivate students.

▶ Learning from the blackboard provides an alternative to looking at the book.

▶ The blackboard provides a focus for all the class to learn from.

▶ Charts on the blackboard provide lots of guided speaking and writing practice.

▶ Always clean the blackboard before the next lesson.

You remember we asked you to redraw a muddled blackboard layout. Figure 19.10 shows one possible way of making the information clear and easier to learn from.

Figure 19.10

Classroom Action Task

Think of a lesson you will be teaching next week:

- Write down the new language your students will learn and mark any arrows, boxes or underlining that will help.

- Draw up a blackboard plan, showing the divisions and exactly what you will write, and where.

- Before your lesson, practise your blackboard plan in your classroom.

20/Using Resources

We saw in the last chapter why resources are important to help students learn better and how we can use the blackboard more effectively.

In this chapter, we will look at what resources we have, or we can find or make, and how different resources can be used for many different teaching and learning techniques. We suggest activities for using them to bring variety to your classroom. There are also tips on how to store and share these resources.

WHAT RESOURCES ARE THERE IN THE CLASSROOM?

Resources are books, any person, animal, plant or any object, that make teaching and learning easier, clearer and more interesting.

Look around your classroom. Maybe you have a room with four walls, floor and ceiling with windows and a door. This room probably has a blackboard and a desk and tables and chairs and a cupboard. This room also possibly has electricity, so there is a light, maybe a fan or a heater. Maybe your classroom is outside, under a tree, and the students sit on the ground, and you write on the ground with a stick. All these things are teaching and learning resources. We use many different kinds of resources to improve motivation and student participation. Using resources makes learning more realistic and helps students understand. It is much more helpful to hold a real orange in your hands when you are asking the price of that orange, or offering to sell the orange to someone, or asking about its shape or colour.

FINDING AND MAKING RESOURCES

Finding and using resources can be time consuming; however, it does not take much time to:

▶ ask students to bring the packaging from some food to class;
▶ use classroom furniture and fittings;
▶ bring a bag of vegetables into class;
▶ ask students to put something from their school bag on their desk;
▶ draw a selection of fruit on the blackboard;
▶ find a magazine with pictures;
▶ find a newspaper in English;
▶ draw a picture on a flashcard;
▶ invite a colleague into the class for ten minutes.

All teachers have certain resources in their immediate teaching environment. There is also another world outside the classroom, where teachers and students lead their daily lives. Everyone has access to the home, the street, the shops and the market, and all these have a variety of resources. One difference between language students in different parts of the world is the amount of English that is available to them in their everyday world. For example:

▶ How many people who you know and meet speak some English?
▶ Are there radio and television broadcasts in English?
▶ Is there easy and cheap access to films and videos in English?
▶ Are there affordable newspapers, magazines and books, or are they accessible in libraries?
▶ Is there written English anywhere, in the form of street names, shop signs, food and goods packaging?

In class, students can, as part of the learning process, with your help, label with English names the furniture and equipment, and make wall charts, word games, dictionary boxes. At home, teachers and students can ask their families to find old clothes, household items, packaging, toys, equipment. On the street and in the shops, teachers and students can note down or find food packaging, bags, signs, advertising, postcards, tourist information, airline information, bus and train information, bank and post office leaflets (Figure 20.1).

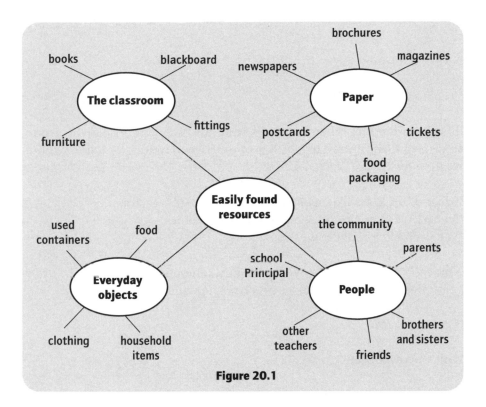

Figure 20.1

USING STUDENTS AS A RESOURCE

Students often wear different clothes to school. Even if there is a school uniform, there are small variations in colour or style. You can use to advantage the different heights of students. So students themselves are a good source for talking about similarities, differences and comparisons, such as:

'Her skirt is darker than mine.'
'My socks are longer than his.'
'I'm the tallest in the class.'

Students come from different families, who may have different ideas and opinions. All this information can easily and usefully be gathered by students in the form of class questionnaires, surveys, interviews and presentations. You can use unusual pictures, or, with higher-level students, controversial statements to elicit their reactions and ideas and to let them imagine what they would feel like in the same situation.

Students can find out likes and dislikes. To have lots of practice with the structures, they can practise questions and answers like:

'Do you like . . . ?'

with the responses:

'Yes I do' or 'No I don't'.

This information, when collected from all the class, in pair or group work, can then be used to give lots of practice in writing or talking about relative quantities, such as:

'Most of the class like bananas, but few of us like carrots.'
'My friend likes rice but he doesn't like potatoes.'
'We both like oranges.'

You can show pictures, or you or the students can demonstrate or draw examples of physical skills, to practise language:

'Can you swim?'

with the responses

'Yes I can' or 'No I can't'.

USING OBJECTS AS A RESOURCE

You will remember that in Chapter 4 we explained how to present and practise new language using real objects ('Could you lend me a pencil?' and 'Could you open the door?'). Students can also use ordinary objects as props or to help when speaking dialogues or role-plays, for example:

► Stones or seeds can be used as money or counters.
► A broom can be a guitar, a microphone or a crutch.
► A bin can be used as a hat or a house or an animal.
► A blackboard rubber can be used as a phone, a sandwich, or a remote control.
► A length of cloth can be clothing, headwear, a room divider, a shop front, a table cover, curtains, or bedding.

Students can use real objects to make a shop or a room where they can practise new language in an appropriate environment. At first students may get excited or confused when there are real objects to touch, different learning resources to look at and respond to. However, if you use resources regularly, then students will soon come to accept and look forward to learning from them.

You can put some small objects into a bag for each group and students can take turns to feel one object in the bag, and without looking at it, describe it to their group. The winner has the next turn.

Ask students to each bring a favourite object to school. In groups, students can talk about the history of their object, why it is their favourite. Then they can make up stories around their group's set of objects.

WAYS TO SHARE BOOKS

Sometimes there may be only one book for the whole class, or not enough books to allow for one book for each student. However, there are ways to share this book and the information and ideas in it.

Give the important parts of the textbook by:

▶ copying the relevant parts, questions or story onto the blackboard before the lesson for the students to copy into their notebooks, or to read and give spoken or written answers;
▶ dictating exercises that students can then complete;
▶ asking questions to guide the students towards understanding the whole story, while you write or draw words or pictures to guide and remind students.

You, or students in turn, can read the story, questions or information aloud, which is good listening practice for other students. They can then use questions and answers to check understanding, and possibly you or a student can write or dictate the important information on the blackboard for future reference.

If the only book is a set literature text, then again there are several ways to share the information. This is an opportunity to usefully set up reading groups with specific tasks.

It may be necessary to divide the book *carefully* into its separate chapters or pages. This sounds drastic but it is for a good reason, as it gets the book to the students. Make sure each chapter is carefully and safely put in a plastic bag or a file. Depending on the size of your class and the number of chapters in the book, divide the class into groups so that each group has one chapter to work on. If you have a large class or a book with few pages, you can separate each page and give a page to each student, pair of students or group of students, depending on the number in your class. Monitors are responsible for distributing and collecting chapters or pages and returning them to the correct order. The information gathered from the separate chapters can be put on a wall chart, in note form for each chapter.

Another way to share a limited number of books is to rotate book with other work. This means that one group will be working on the book, maybe in a quiet corner of the classroom or at the back, while you do something else with the rest of the class. This means that at some point you will have to help that particular reading group catch up. This could be done in the form of a class revision exercise, where the rest of the class has to demonstrate what they learned.

Set literature texts can be a good source of listening practice, when the teacher, or students in turn, read aloud some of the story. Again the important 'Wh . . . ?' facts can be elicited from the class, and students in turn put the facts into a wall chart.

COLLECTING, MAKING, RE-USING AND SHARING RESOURCES

One resource you can collect is used food packaging. You can talk about the English that is written on it. The plain back of this card packaging is also very useful. You can write activity instructions for role plays on a square of card, which keeps longer than a piece of paper. You can stick pictures onto this card, or draw objects or write words for flashcards so that you have cues for drills. Another simple but useful resource is simply a big piece of paper or card with a word written on it, or a picture drawn on it, which is large enough for all students to read.

Flashcards are used to

► prompt drills (for example if you are practising requests, a picture of a shop could produce the language 'Can you go to the shop?');
► ask for suggestions about the characters or process of a story;
► ask for thoughts about a picture or a situation;
► prompting 'Yes' or 'No' answers to questions, or questions from statements (with 'Yes', 'No' or '?' on the cards).

Flashcards mean that you can do some drawings in advance, and re-use them in a single or a series of lessons.

You can use resources in many different ways, for different levels and to teach different topics in different lessons. For example, food packaging can be used for shopping games, prices, numbers, countries, food likes and dislikes, recipes, shapes, colours, ingredients or manufacturing processes.

Make a note of how you used each resource. If you get into the habit of doing this immediately after the lesson, it will not take long. Make quick notes during the lesson and write it out clearly at the end of the day. Keep this useful information really short. If it is too long you will not write it and no other teacher will want to read it. If you leave this task until the next day, you will probably forget, as the lesson will not be fresh in your mind. This brief but useful task is like planning each lesson, which can be a bit of a challenge at first, but with daily practice it takes very little time and it is a very useful guide. Keep the information with the relevant resource.

It is a good idea to start a sharing scheme with other teachers. Come to an agreement with colleagues, where you give one to them, if you are given one. To start other teachers using resources, offer to go through an idea with them, or let them observe part of your lesson, using some new resources.

How to Make and Use Visual Aids, by Nicola Harford and Nicola Baird, published by VSO, 1997 (see p. 166) has many more ideas on making and using resources for teaching and learning language.

ORGANISING AND STORING RESOURCES

If you are going to share resources with other teachers, you need to make a written list of what is available. No one will use these resources unless it is easy to find what they want. Make a notebook into an advance signing-out list, giving the name, the date, the time and the resource that will be taken. This simple system helps to avoid argument or disappointment.

Make your resource collection as long-lasting as possible, by putting them in bags or sticking them onto pieces of card. Organising and storing resources for re-use is much easier if they are packed safely and clearly and ordered with easy-to-see labels. You can re-use plastic or paper or cloth shopping bags if necessary to store the resources, closed with clothes-pegs. You need to label and store each resource package in an easily accessible, but secure, cupboard or shelf. If your box of resources looks like rubbish it may get accidentally thrown away, so mark it very clearly as 'Teaching Resources'.

To ensure all the teachers in your school know about, contribute to and use teaching and learning resources, you can arrange occasional workshops with colleagues to:

▶ discuss how you all use the resources;
▶ co-ordinate collecting of resources;
▶ share ideas for making resources;
▶ organise a session for making resources together.

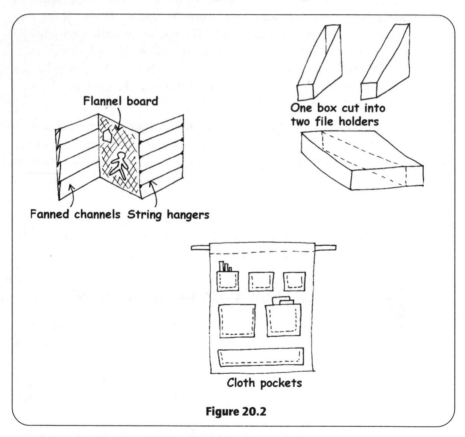

Flannel board

One box cut into two file holders

Fanned channels String hangers

Cloth pockets

Figure 20.2

MAKING THE CLASSROOM A WORLD OF ENGLISH

Some of the resources you and your students collect or make can become a permanent fixture in your classroom. Call this area the English corner. This constant and varied access to English helps students become more familiar with English.

To create a world of English, pin up any newspapers or magazines in English, from or about England or any English-speaking country. You can start your own class library with any books you find or are given. Use packaging items for a 'shop' arranged on a shelf, or a series of boxes to look like a shop, where students can simply look and learn or play shop-keeper and customer-language games in spare moments or as a planned part of a lesson. Travel brochures and posters can be pinned up for students to talk about and possibly to annotate with vocabulary or questions. Cinema and theatre posters, in English or students' first language, and pictures, can be pinned up, or students can draw their own posters. Students can write comments or a review of the play or film they have seen, or a book that they have read, together with a book-cover illustrating part of the story. Other students can add their own opinions.

Picture and word wall charts can be made and pinned on the wall, or hung up on clothes-lines with pegs. These charts can explain and illus-trate the new vocabulary, tenses and language structures that are learnt over the term. To encourage good work, and provide a model of good English, you can select or vote to display a selection of students' work for a week or a month.

If you have access to a cassette player and any cassettes in English, you can make a cassette listening corner. A pair of headphones will make the task quieter, but pairs or groups will need to learn to listen quietly. The task could be to write down the words to a song or a speech, but as this can be quite a challenge, getting the general idea, of 'Who/What/When/Where/Why/How?', is a good general listening technique to teach and practice.

Classroom Action Task

Find some resources and think how you could use them to make teaching and learning more interesting and memorable.

Prepare these resources for the classroom.

Practise using these resources, how to hold them easily, while talking, moving and showing them to all the class.

Try these resources out in a well-planned lesson.

After the lesson, write a few brief comments on how this lesson went in your Teacher's Action Diary, and tell a colleague what you did.

Package and store this resource-package for future use.

Encourage colleagues to use your idea, and also to share an idea with you.

AND FINALLY . . .

Many VSO teachers, their colleagues and teachers from around the world, contributed the ideas in this book. They have faced many of the challenges that you face, and we hope that the methods, approaches and activities in this book will help and inspire you in your classroom.

Further Reading

Crystal, D. *Discover Grammar*. Addison Wesley Longman Education, 1996.

Bolitho, R. and Tomlinson, B. *Discover English*. Heinemann, 1980.

Doff, A. *Teach English*. Cambridge University Press, 1988.

Edge, J. *Mistakes and Correction*. Longman, 1989.

Frank, C. and Rinvolucri, M. *Grammar in Action Again*. Prentice-Hall International Language Teaching, 1991.

*Hadfield, J. and Hadfield, C. *Simple Speaking Activities*. Oxford University Press, 1999.

*Hadfield, J. and Hadfield, C. *Presenting New Language*. Oxford University Press, 1999.

*Hadfield, J. and Hadfield, C. *Simple Listening Activities*. Oxford University Press, 1999.

Harmer, J. *Teaching and Learning Grammar*. Longman, 1987.

Harmer, J. *The Practice of English Language Teaching*. Longman, 1997.

Marsland, B. *Lessons from Nothing*. Cambridge University Press, 1998.

McCarthy, M. and O'Dell, F. *English Vocabulary in Use*. Cambridge University Press, 1997.

Murphy, R. *Essential Grammar in Use With Answers*. Cambridge University Press, 1997.

Roberts, R. *Discover Elementary English Grammar*. MFP Publications, 1997.

Scott, W. A. and Ytreberg, L. H. *Teaching English to Children*. Longman, 1990.

Seligson, P. *Helping Students to Speak*. Richmond, 1997.

Swan, M. *Practical English Usage*. Oxford University Press, 1996.

Swan, K. and Walter, C. *How English Works*. Oxford University Press, 1997.

Tice, J. *The Mixed Ability Class*. Richmond, 1997.

Underwood, M. *Effective Classroom Management*. Longman, 1987.

* These books are in the Oxford Basics series.

VSO Books

VSO Books is the publishing unit of VSO. Since 1958, more than 27,000 skilled volunteers have worked alongside national colleagues in over 60 countries throughout the developing world. VSO Books publishes practical books and Working Papers in education and development based upon current thinking and the wide range of professional experience of volunteers and their overseas partners. Working Papers in Development are published on VSO's web site for free downloading: www.vso.org.uk/pubs/wpapers/

Books for teachers

The Agricultural Science Teachers' Handbook, Peter Taylor, 148pp, 160 illustrations, VSO Books, ISBN 0 9509050 7 0.

A Handbook for Teaching Sports, National Coaching Foundation, VSO/Heinemann, 160pp, ISBN 0 435 92320 X.

How to Make and Use Visual Aids, Nicola Harford, Nicola Baird, VSO/Heinemann, 128pp, ISBN 0 435 92317 X.

Introductory Technology: A Resource Book, Adrian Owens, VSO/ITP, 142pp, ISBN 1 85339 064 X.

The Maths Teachers' Handbook, Jane Portman, Jeremy Richardson, VSO/Heinemann, 108pp, ISBN 0 435 92318 8.

Participatory Forestry – The Process of Change in India and Nepal, Mary Hobley, 338pp, VSO/ODI, ISBN 0 85003 204 0.

The Science Teachers' Handbook, Andy Byers, Ann Childs, Chris Lainé, VSO/Heinemann, 144pp, ISBN 0 435 92302 1.

Setting Up and Running a School Library, Nicola Baird, VSO/Heinemann, 144pp, ISBN 0 435 2304 8 4.

Books for development workers

Adult Literacy: A Handbook for Development Workers, Paul Fordham, Deryn Holland, Juliet Millican, VSO/Oxfam Publications, 192pp, ISBN 0 85598 315 9.

Care and Safe Use of Hospital Equipment, Muriel Skeet, David Fear, VSO Books, 188pp, ISBN 0 9509050 5 4.

Culture, Cash and Housing, Andy Bevan, Maurice Mitchell, VSO/ITP, 128pp, ISBN 1 85339 153 0.

Diagnosis and Treatment: A Training Manual for Primary Health Care Workers, Keith Birrell and Ginny Birrell, VSO/Macmillan, 272 pp, ISBN 0 333 72211 6.

How to Grow a Balanced Diet, Ann Burgess, Grace Maina, Philip Harris, Stephanie Harris, VSO Books, 244pp, ISBN 0 9509050 6 2.

Made in Africa, Janet Leek, Andrew Scott, Matthew Taylor, VSO/ITP, 70pp, ISBN 1 85339 214 6.

Managing for a Change: How to Run Community Development Projects, Anthony Davies, ITP, 160pp, ISBN 1 85339 339 1.

Water Supplies for Rural Communities, Colin and Mog Ball, VSO/ITP, 56pp, ISBN 1 85339 112 3.

Using Technical Skills in Community Development, Jonathan Dawson, ed. Mog Ball, VSO/ITP, 64pp, ISBN 1 85339 078 X.

To order and for more information, contact:
VSO Books, 317 Putney Bridge Road, London SW15 2PN, UK.
Tel: +44 20 8780 7200   fax: +44 20 8780 7300.
web site: www.vso.org.uk

Index